INTEROCEANIC CANALS

AN ESSAY

ON THE

QUESTION OF LOCATION FOR A SHIP CANAL

ACROSS THE

AMERICAN CONTINENT.

BY HENRY STUCKLE,

Late General Superintendent of the Alsacian Railroads; Author of "Voies de Communication aux Etats Unis," Paris, 1847.

With a Chart of the World on Mercator's Projection, and a Map of the Southern part of the Isthmus of Tehuantepec.

NEW YORK:
D. VAN NOSTRAND, 23 MURRAY & 27 WARREN STS.
LONDON:
B. F. STEVENS, 17 HENRIETTA STREET, COVENT GARDEN.
PARIS:
E. DENTU, PALAIS ROYAL, GALERIE D'ORLEANS, 17 AND 19.

MDCCCLXX.

A. CARR & CO., PRINTERS,
42 Cortlandt Street, N. Y.

CONTENTS.

PREFACE.

One of the most remarkable of the progressive movements of our time is that which tends to perfect more and more our means of intercommunication and to reduce distances, and the questions thereby created often excite universal interest.

The two most important problems of this nature, which the genius of man has been called upon to solve, are beyond contradiction the penetration of that isthmus which separated the Mediterranean sea and the Indian ocean, and of the other, the opening of which would unite the waters of the Atlantic and Pacific. The solution of the first of these problems is already accomplished; that of the second is to-day projected. To this latter these pages are mainly devoted.

As a proper introduction to the consideration of the question, I have thought it advisable to present a general view of the subject of interoceanic communication in America. I have followed this with an account of the history and construction of the Suez canal, and have spoken of the economical results which it is destined to produce upon the commerce of the world. After this, I have treated, by way of comparison, the analogous work which it is proposed to construct in our hemisphere, examining it throughout from the point of view of the existing natural resources and the necessary expenses attending construction. I have also considered the conditions under which the American canal would necessarily be operated and the special advantages which it would realize.

The developement of these several subjects lead to the discussion of the system of construction to be adopted, and the location to be selected, at one point of the Isthmus rather than at another. The arguments presented in this discussion in favor of a locality, situated more to the north than Darien, have acquired still greater strength to-day, if possible, since the failure of the expedition lately undertaken by the Federal Government with a view to the discovery in that latitude of a convenient passage for the projected canal.

Another fact renders the publication of this essay, written some five months since, still more timely and *apropos*; this is the recent vote of Congress,* appropria-

* At a meeting of the American Society of Civil Engineers on April 16th, 1870, Col. Julius W. Adams read a paper on "*American Interoceanic Ship-Canals,*" after which the subject was open to discussion, and General J. G. Barnard moved and the society

"*Resolved*, that in the opinion of the American Society of Civil Engineers, the relations of the isthmus of Tehuantepec to the United States are so peculiar and so different from those of any other suggested route for canal or transit, that it is highly important that the patronage and influence of the Government, and the capital of its citizens, should not be committed to any ship-canal or transit enterprise until the practicability or non-practicability of a canal across that isthmus has been determined by a survey to be made for that object."

Two days after, Hon. R. E. Fenton submitted to the Senate, and had referred to its Committee on Foreign Affairs, the following:

"WHEREAS, the commerce of the world, and more especially that of the western hemisphere, renders it important that a ship-canal should be constructed across the American isthmus; and

WHEREAS, the Government of the Republic of Mexico has conceded to an American company the privilege of opening interoceanic communication. by means of a railway across the isthmus of Tehuantepec, and now proposes to add thereto a concession for a ship-canal; therefore be it

Resolved, that the President of the United States shall obtain the assent of the Government of Mexico, then the Secretary of War is hereby authorized to detail a corps of engineers to make a survey of the summit of the isthmus of Tehuantepec to ascertain if there be sufficient water at the summit of said isthmus for a ship-canal; and if it should be found, on examination, that there is sufficient water, then a survey of the isthmus for a ship-canal shall be made from the Gulf of Mexico to the Pacific ocean, together with the complete plan proposed and estimates for the same, under such regulations and with such provisions, as the Committee on Foreign Relations may recommend."

This resolution was favorably reported by the Committee and on the proposition of Hon. Charles Sumner, Chairman of said committee, Congress, on the 12th of July, 1870, appropriated $30,000 for surveys to be made upon the isthmuses of Tehuantepec and Nicargua for the purpose of ascertaining the respective practicability of these localities for the construction of an interoceanic ship-canal.

ting funds for explorations to be made, under Government auspices, at Nicaragua and Tehuantepec, in order to ascertain the respective conditions presented by these localities for the construction of an interoceanic ship-canal. The details which I have given will acquaint the reader with the results of the previous investigations which have been made to this end upon the isthmus of Tehuantepec, and will enable him to form a judgment of the favorable expectations entertained with reference to the latter region in view of the projected work.

The ample figures and statistical tables quoted in the pages of this publication, are, as far as possible, from official sources. Finally, I have striven to leave nothing to be desired, either in the substance or the form of the book, and, with reference to the latter, my labors have been greatly assisted by those of my *collaborateur*, Mr. William O. Stoddard of New York, to whom I would express my grateful acknowledgment.

HENRY STUCKLE.

New York, August, 1870.

CHAPTER FIRST.

Present State of Interoceanic Communication in America.

It is nearly four hundred years since Christopher Columbus, following the indications of previous geographers, sought to find a shorter route to Asia and, by steering west, to reach the Orient. In the course of his explorations he discovered a new continent, which, up to the very hour of his death, he continued to regard as Asia. He never suspected that he had then before him a barrier which it would be necessary to penetrate in order to reach the Indies, and that he had still to overcome a distance greater than that which he had traversed in order to accomplish his grand discovery.

In 1513, when Columbus had been in his grave but seven years, Nuñez de Balbóa first saw the Pacific ocean (called for many years the "South sea"), from the mountain tops of Panama, and, after it had been otherwise established that there existed an ocean "even more vast than the Atlantic," an enthusiastic emulation arose among men of enterprise, who had been made illustrious by their discoveries in this hemisphere, to find a navigable passage across the central portion of the new world.

Juan Dias de Solis was ordered in 1515 to search for that passage supposed to exist through the straits. A few years later, in 1522, four vessels having been built at Panama, Avila and the pilot Niño set out to explore the coast of the Pacific from the Bay of San Miguel to the Gulf of Fonseca, expecting to find at the latter place a passage by water through to the Gulf of Honduras. The same year, Cortez, after having subdued the empire of Montezuma, set himself to work exploring with the view to find a natural water passage. Four ships were built at Zacatula, two for direct trade to the Moluccas and two to search for the strait. The voyage to the Moluccas was postponed; but the search for the strait was prosecuted so vigorously that, between the expedition of Avila and his own, every inlet was explored from Colima in 18½° Lat. N. down to the Bay of San Miguel, a distance of above 2500 miles of coast line, but of course without finding any passage.

On the Atlantic coast, the course of the river Goatzacoalcos emptying into the Gulf of Mexico, and penetrating with its affluents deep into the interior of the isthmus of Tehuantepec, was examined with special care. All these fruitless researches made known the important fact that water communication between the two seas was impossible except by an artificial passage.

In the meantime the policy of Spain underwent a change. Charles V, by the treaty of Saragossa, mortgaged the Moluccas to the King of Portugal, who had just married his sister, and the trade of the Moluccas passing for a time out of the hands of the Spaniards, there was no immediate pressure for the construction of a transit across the Isthmus.* Under Philip II the idea was revived. Two Flemish Engineers made surveys for a ship canal upon the isthmus of Panama, but a short time afterwards the subject was once more abandoned. If Cortez, Grijalva, the Cabots, and so many other heroes, who dreamed for the next century the construction of some isthmian canal, could return to the world, what would be their astonishment to see the great question almost in the same condition as when they left the theatre of their exploits.

EARLY PROJECTS.

It would be too tedious, and foreign to our purpose, to follow, step by step, the various causes which during the three subsequent centuries, in which Spain was absolute master of the central regions of America, prevented any decisive action

---

*Historical and geographical notes on the earliest discoveries in America by Henry Stevens of Vermont F. S. A, etc (*The American Journal of Science and Arts, New Haven. November*, 1869.)

towards the construction of an interoceanic communication so useful to the whole human race. Towards the end of his reign, Philip II, actuated by that narrow, mean and envious commercial policy which had long characterized the course of the Spanish government, issued a decree forbidding all surveys and explorations in the future, having for object the means of connecting the two oceans. Antonio de Alcedo, who wrote a geographical and historical work on the West Indies, which was published in 1786, and subsequently suppressed by the Spanish Government "on account of the information it might give to foreign powers," gives this fact, and furthermore says that the navigation of the river San Miguel, the Atrato, and other rivers, situated upon the isthmus, was prohibited on pain of death.

A century passed away inertly. War was waged between England and Spain, swarms of buccaneers crowded the Caribbean Sea, Jamaica was conquered, and from Port Royal harbor bold adventurers, who were nothing less than pirates, sailed forth to prey upon the Spanish colonies. Dampier crossed the isthmus and marched into the interior in search of gold. The question of an easy passage from one sea to the other was not one of the smallest anxieties of these enterprising people, and we possess to this day the record of their surveys, for example, that of the bar of the river Goatzacoalcos.

Alarmed at the boldness of the buccaneers, the Spanish monarch issued a decree in 1685, closing by destruction the gold mines of Darien in the vicinity of rivers, "because the coveting of them has induced the pirates to undertake the transit from the sea of the North to the sea of the South, by these rivers, to the prejudice of the public cause."

It must not be imagined that during the following century absolutely nothing was done towards finding or constructing a passage between the two oceans. Carrera made an expedition which failed miserably, but Milla, a Spanish officer, crossed once. He left the river Savana at Principe, moving directly across the country, ascending the ravines of the Andes to the headwaters of the Sucubti, thence down the sinuous Chucuanque to the ocean. It was also proposed by engineers, to the Court of Madrid, to use the river Chagres as the medium of communication. But Spain was no longer the great power she once had been. True, she still was the mistress of Mexico and all of Central and the greater part of South America. Her material strength, however, had been wasted in worse than insane wars in Europe and in revolutions at home. Portugal made some efforts, but without success, and Great Britain was at war with France and her American colonies as well as with other powers during a great part of the century.

The great utility of such an undertaking as the opening of an artificial way through the narrows of Central America, became still more evident toward the latter part of the eighteenth century, which witnessed the rising importance of Hindostan, China, and of the islands of the Indian ocean, as well as the discovery of Australia and the numerous islands of the Pacific. The length of time required and the danger incurred in doubling the two tempestuous capes by which alone the passage could be effected, served continually to keep attention fixed on the inestimable advantages which would accrue from an easy interoceanic communication.

At the same epoch the Spanish Americans became restive under the rule of the mother country. Some time in 1790 General Francisco Miranda, one of the earliest martyrs of South American independence, proposed to M. Pitt, the Prime Minister of Great Britain, a project for a ship canal, "as a means to the emancipation of the Spanish colonies and a furtherance of British commerce in the southern and eastern seas." A few years later he held a conference in Paris with prominent men, and the result was a proposition now on file in the archives of the British Foreign Office, to send an armament of 10,000 men and a fleet, jointly with Great Britain, and take possession of the isthmus of Darien. M. Pitt lent a favorable ear to this second proposition, which would most probably have been carried into effect had not the vacillating policy of President Adams prevented its acceptance.

In the midst of these complications, Spain, whose policy seemed to have become more liberal, made a last effort in behalf of the establishment of an interoceanic transit. This was in 1774, when the Viceroy of Mexico ordered new explorations upon the isthmus of Tehuantepec. These explorations demonstrated the feasability of a ship canal from the Pacific to the Goatzacoalcos, by which navigation could be continued to the Gulf of Mexico. In 1814 the construction of the canal was formally decreed by the Cortes, but, as usual with that august body, they were just in time to be too late, the revolt of the colonies rendering such an enterprise impossible at that period.

MODERN PROJECTS.

To Humboldt the world is indebted for much valuable information regarding routes for connecting the oceans, and, it may also be said, for reviving among nations possessing extensive commercial relations, an active interest in the solution of the great problem. His plans embraced five distinct routes, which were afterwards so divided as to form the basis of some twenty projects, as enumerated by Rear-Admiral C. H. Davis, in his Report to the Secretary of the Navy, in 1866, of which we have availed ourselves for the purposes of our description.

In these latter days, when the public mind is occupied with the question of interoceanic communication across our continent, some of our leading journals have furnished detailed descriptions of the more prominent of these projects. We shall therefore only present here, in a condensed form, the chief features of the principal plans proposed, enumerating them in the order of their geographical position from north to south.

TEHUANTEPEC.

It would seem, from the manner in which Admiral Davis refers to this isthmus in his Report, that he is inclined to exclude it from the general discussion of existing canal projects.

Certainly, if we confine our consideration to the transverse section of the isthmus of Tehuantepec, annexed to the Report of Admiral Davis, we should be led to approve, without being too positive, the conclusion to which he comes, viz: "From this survey we learn that this route possesses but little merit as a practicable line for the construction of a ship canal." But the profile here referred to, is that of the survey for the construction of a railway, made under the direction of Major (afterwards Major-General) J. G. Barnard. An examination of the results of the exploration made in 1843, by Mr. G. Moro, with a view to the construction of a canal, would have undoubtedly led to the formation of a more correct opinion of the availability of that isthmus for establishing artificial water communication. The line projected measured from 160 to 170 miles, but the actual length of *canal* required to unite the Atlantic and Pacific is but fifty miles. This canal, after traversing the large lagoons situated upon the southern coast of the isthmus, connects with the Goatzacoalcos near its point of confluence with the Malatengo, and from thence the communication with the Gulf of Mexico is effected by utilizing the former great river. As we shall have, in the course of this essay, to furnish a detailed description of the explorations made to demonstrate the practicability of a canal at Tehuantepec, we need not, at this point, dwell at greater length upon the subject. That which we have already said is sufficient to make known the existence of the project, and to correct, if necessary, the unfavorable opinion which the employment of Major Barnard's map, as applicable to a canal, would be likely to create.

NICARAGUA.

The greatest scheme of Central American canalization which has ever been advocated, is that passing through Nicaragua, where the comparative facilities for forming a magnificent canal for ships of the largest size admit of no dispute, but if from no other consideration, the gigantic nature of the enterprise and its enormous cost must place it, if not beyond reach, at all events in a problematic position, when we consider the data obtained up to the present time.

In 1830 a company was formed in Holland under the patronage of the King with the view of constructing the canal, but the disturbances in that country broke up the company. In 1835 the project was brought before the Government of the United States and a resolution was passed by the Senate in its favor, but the agent sent by General Jackson, then President, to arrange with the Nicaraguan authorities, died on the road, and the matter was allowed to drop. Some time later, attempts were made by Americans to establish a canal at Nicaragua, but without any perceptible result. No one has taken so warm an interest in the subject as the present Emperor of the French. Don Francisco Castillon, Envoy to the court of France, put himself in communication, in 1840, with Prince Louis Napoleon Bonaparte, at that time a prisoner at Ham, and proposed to him in the name of the Nicaraguan Government to take upon himself exclusively the construction of the proposed canal. Had this offer been accepted the result might have been that Louis Napoleon would have ruled the destinies of Nicaragua instead of those of France; but, fortunately for the latter country, the captive was not allowed to go. A decree of the Government of Nicaragua, dated January 8th, 1846, assigned to the future enterprise the name of "Canale Napoleone de Nicaragua," and M. de Marcoleta, Chargé d'Affaires of Nicaragua in Holland, was authorized to conclude with the Prince a treaty which should confer upon him all the powers necessary to organize in Europe a company for the execution of the undertaking.* Some very interesting correspondence passed between the Prince and Señor Castillon, and the subject appears to have made so permanent an impression upon the mind of the former, that, after his arrival in England, he devoted a considerable amount of time and study to it, and not only wrote a most able pamphlet, but publicly advocated the subject at the Institute of Civil Engineers in London.†

* Oeuvres de Napoleon III. vol. 2, page 472.

† Minutes of proceedings of the Institute of Civil Engineers vol. VI. page 427.

The fact that in crossing the isthmus, the river San Juan and the lake of Nicaragua can be utilized, gives to this line at first sight something of attraction. Lake Nicaragua and the San Juan are both navigable, and their water communications reduce the isthmus to one tenth of its whole breadth and the surrounding region of country cannot be surpassed in agricultural and mineral resources. But to counter-balance these advantages, there are topographical obstacles existing upon the narrow part of the isthmus to be traversed by the canal, and which are difficult of removal. Various lines have been proposed from the lake to the Pacific outlet. Three of these pass through lake Managua, a fourth, going partly along the Rio Grande, terminates at Brito, a fifth at San Juan del Sur, a sixth proceeds by the Sapoa river to Salinas bay, a seventh, keeping on the southern part of the State of Nicaragua, proposes to cut from the river San Juan through the State of Costa Rica to Nicoya gulf. Two of these routes, those of San Juan and Brito, have been surveyed.

The description of the survey of the former, made by Lieut. I. Bailey, is given by the excellent book of Commander Bedford Pim, " the Gate of the Pacific" to which we are indebted for a part of our information on Nicaraguan projects. The whole length of the proposed canal from the Lake to San Juan del Sur is 15 miles. According to the plan, in the first eight miles only one lock is necessary. In the next mile 64 feet of lockage are required, in the next three miles there are about two miles of deep cutting and one mile of tunnel, and then a descent of 200 feet in three miles by lockage to the Pacific.

Messrs. Child and Fay surveyed in 1850-51 the line to Brito for the American Atlantic and Pacific Ship Canal Company. An easy route of 194 miles in length was selected. It traverses the lake directly to its outlet at Port San Carlos, and employs slack water navigation in the San Juan for a distance exceeding ninety miles, and then pursues a canal independent of the river to the lake. The proposed plan comprises twenty-eight locks between the Pacific ocean and the Caribbean sea, two artificial harbors and extensive improvements in the way of excavations, piers, jetties, break waters, etc. The labor required by both the projected routes would be enormous. It is, however, to be considered that the other lines proposed have not yet been actually surveyed, and it is possible that a line may yet be discovered which will solve the problem that has been the subject of more or less earnest study since 1830.

A new fact has lately come to light to revive the hope of an easy final solution. M. Michel Chevalier, whose high authority in matters of science and industry offers a strong guaranty, has obtained from the governments of Nicaragua and Costa Rica a concession for the construction of a ship canal across the isthmus. Careful explorations will be made to determine the question of the most advantageous location of the line, as well with reference to comparative cost as to facility of working. In a letter recently addressed by M. Chevalier to the author of this essay, he expresses the greatest confidence in the successful result of his labors, and everything seems to indicate that, compared with what is at present known concerning the projects south of Nicaragua, the cost of execution at the latter point would be smaller. From this we see that the question of the Nicaragua route is yet to be determined, whatever may be said.

PANAMA.

More attention has been attracted to this portion of the Isthmus, and to that part of it adjoining the main-land of South America, than to any other, because it offers the *narrowest* barrier between the two seas. Of the various projects proposed, perhaps that of connecting the river Chagres and Rio Grande by a short canal, and then deepening their beds, has been the most favorably received. The line has been thoroughly examined, but the nature of the country did not come up to expectation, and the plan has been consequently abandoned.

The French Government, under Louis Philippe, manifested a decided predilection for the Panama line, and caused it, in 1843, to be minutely surveyed to ascertain a route for a canal, by M. Napoleon Garella, a distinguished engineer, whose scientific operations in the Pyrenees had added greatly to his reputation. He proposed to start from the little bay of Vaca del Monte, twelve miles west of Panama, and cross over to Limon bay, two miles and a half east of Chagres, the summit to be tunnelled through at least three miles from end to end. He estimated the cost at $25,000,000, the canal to have twenty-three feet in depth and forty-six feet in width. The highest elevation of the canal was 460 feet above the sea. The descent from the summit level to the Pacific was to be made by means of seventeen locks, which would be much crowded together. On the Atlantic side the descent was to be effected by eighteen locks, more conveniently located. Independently of the necessity of constructing a tunnel of dimensions as yet unknown, and the great cost of the undertaking, the project does not present satisfactory conditions of water supply, and a considerable sum is required for the construction of harbors at the two terminations, nature not having provided them at these points. All these different reasons have cast a chill upon the expectations which had been conceived. It is true that engineering investigations have demonstrated the possibility of the solution of the problem, but nothing has been accomplished in the domain of realization.

DARIEN.

There are three other localities which command great attention. These three routes are from San Blas or Mandonga bay to river Chepo or Bayamo, flowing into the Pacific; from Caledonia bay to the Gulf of San Miguel, and from the southern part of the Gulf of Darien to the Gulf of San Miguel.

In 1864 Mr. Fred. Kelley, of New York, surveyed the route from the Gulf of San Blas to Chepo. He found the harbor of San Blas "spacious and deep," while, on the Pacific side, the channel of the Chepo had "not less than eighteen feet of water at mean low tide." A canal in this direction would require a tunnel of about the length of that of Mount Cenis, (seven miles) through the Alps. The canal would be a "thorough cut" about thirty miles long.

The next line, from Caledonia bay to the Gulf of San Miguel, which at both ends presents harbors "spacious and admirable in every respect," has been partly explored by Commander Prevost and Dr. Cullen. That which the latter gentleman has published with relation to this route seems to be very encouraging to the construction of a canal without lockage. His plan would be to unite the waters of the Atlantic, at Caledonia bay, with those of the Savana, flowing into the Gulf of San Miguel.*

A line has been suggested, in 1865, by Mr. De la Charme, from the southern part of the Gulf of Darien to the Gulf of San Miguel, by way of the river Tuyra. According to him, the chain of the Andes is depressed to an elevation of about 58 meters, (about 190 feet) above the main level of tide-water, and the distance between the waters navigable for canoes, on both sides of the chain, was only three miles; but since that

---

* We quote, as to the probable cost of the undertaking, the following paragraph from a memoir concerning this project, presented in 1868 to the Society of Engineers in London :

"There are as yet no data upon which an estimate of the cost of the work could be framed. A rough approximate calculation has, however, been made under the following circumstances. The author having, in 1857, presented all the plans and documents bearing in the matter, to the Emperor of the French, His Majesty, after examining them, forwarded them to Count Walewsky, who appointed a commission of Engineers of the Corps des Ponts et Chaussées, to study the question. The result at which they arrived, after an investigation which occupied three weeks, was that the canal was practicable without a tunnel, and could be completed for 150,000,000 francs. The estimate drawn up, is as follows :

Excavation of the canal	Fr. 76,027,437.25
Dredging of the Savanah	3,080,000.00
Aqueducts	490,000.00
Turning the course of the river	1,241,660.00
Machinery, locks, &c.	38,176,080.00
Material, buildings, tools, clearing forest, and expenses of administration	19,400,000.00
Contingencies	39,584,822.75
	Fr. 178,000,000.00"

It should be noted that these views and estimates are based upon data the exactness of which has been put in doubt by subsequent examinations.

time no scientific statement has been made concerning the conditions which would be required for the construction of the line indicated.

Very recently the results of the explorations of M. L. de Puydt, in Darien, have been published. He claims to have discovered a favorable passage for a canal from the Atlantic, at the port Escondido, following the valleys of the rivers Turgandi and Tanela, and passing over a ridge not more than 46 meters (about 150 feet) above the level of the sea. From thence the line follows the valley of the river Puero and reaches the Tuyra, a confluent of the Savana, which flows into the Bay of San Miguel. M. Puydt projects a canal which would require 88 kilometers (55 miles) of excavation, and 65 kilometers (40 miles) would be navigated in a river which at present has a "depth of from 7 to 20 fathoms." The distance from ocean to ocean will be 158 kilometers (98 miles). The height throughout of the proposed canal, taking the highest and lowest points, presents an average of 11 meters, 90 centimeters (39 feet.) The canal would be 70 meters (230 feet) wide at top and 50 (164 feet) at the bottom. The quantity of earth to be excavated, in order to open the canal, is calculated, according to M. Puydt's indication, to be 125,000,000 cubic meters, or about 163,000,000 cubic yards. There has even been an estimate made of the probable cost of the undertaking, on the hypothesis, that the excavation to be made would consist of 45 per cent. of earth, sand and clay, 35 per cent. rocks, easy to be removed, and 20 per cent. of rock formation, requiring the employment of mining. In adopting this estimate, which is evidently reached in a very superficial manner, the sum required for the whole work would be $70,000,000 ;* that is to say, just as much as has been expended upon the Suez canal.

* 87,800 meters at $600,000 the kilometer	$52,680,000
Allowance of 10 per cent. for any difficulties which may arise in the excavations	5,520,000
Machines, tools, &c.	800,000
Clearing the line	1,000,00C
Expenses of general management for five years	1,000,000

ATRATO BASIN.

The remaining projects take one starting point, namely, the river Atrato, flowing into the Gulf of Darien, which is ascended for same distance and then quitted for one of its affluents, the Napipi or Truando; for example, whence it is proposed to cut a canal to Cupica bay or Kelley's inlet, near the Bay of Panama.

The prominence given to the Atrato valley by Humboldt attracted the attention of Mr. Fred. Kelley of New York, a gentleman whose devotion to the project of connecting the oceans has won for him a foremost position in the ranks of those who have given their time to the subject. To him we are indebted for the first accurate survey of the valley of Atrato. He employed in 1852 Mr. I. C. Trautwine, the well known engineer of Philadelphia, to search for a route. In November of the same year Mr. Trautwine reported a plan for a canal by way of the rivers Atrato and San Juan. Mr. Trautwine proposed to enter the Atrato from the Gulf of Darien through one of its mouths, called Boca Coqueta, ascending it to Quibdo, a distance of 220 miles, thence to ascend the river Quito, a continuation of the Atrato, to the confluence of the Cartiqui and San Pablo; from the latter to the Raspadura and Santa Monica, and from the same to the head of canoe navigation. At this point it was proposed to construct a canal to the river San Juan, which flows into

Agencies in Colombia	100,000
Engineers and superintendence of the work	600,000
Houses, sheds, hospitals	800,000
Sanitary service and medicine	100,000
Extra provisions	400,000
Lamps, levees and wharfs	200,000
Drags	200,000
Ports at each extremity of the canal	200,000
Telegraphs, double wire and exchanges	200,000
Railroads, &c.	2,000,000
Provisions for directors, engineers, agents, instruments, &c.	400,000
Mules	200,000
Ammunition, arms, mining powder	200,000
Steam and sailing vessels to bring provisions	400,000
Accidental expenses	3,000,000
Total	$70,000,000

the Pacific. Several tributaries of the Atrato were examined, including the Pato, the Bando, the Pepe and the Suruco, before selecting the route named. Although he believed this the most practicable line, Mr. Trautwine fairly stated that it was open to serious objections, on account particularly of the extensive and frequent inundations, precluding the possibility of constructing a canal upon a system of dams and locks. It was estimated that the cost of constructing the canal would be 325 million dollars and so the feasibility of the project was destroyed.

During the years 1853 and 1854 other explorations were made under the direction of Mr. Kelly. He caused Mr. James C. Lane to examine the Atrato in hopes of discovering a communication between it and the rivers Andageda, Pato or Bando. Mr. Lane after having ascended, by the Atrato, the river Quibdo, from thence went up the Pato to the head of canoe navigation, and crossed over the country to the navigable waters of the Bando, which he followed for one and three quarter miles; then passing over the dividing ridge he struck the San Juan. This was the route he thought practicable.

While Mr. Lane was thus engaged, Mr. William Kennish was exploring the same valley in another direction. His instructions were to commence operations on the Pacific side, in accordance with what Humboldt had been told, to the effect that "from the Bay of Cupica eastward, for a distance of fifteen or eighteen miles, the ground was level and suitable for a canal, which would terminate in the river Napipi." The representations made to Humboldt stated further that the Cordilleras is entirely broken between this part of the coast and the Atrato valley. Mr. Kennish started along the coast and "to the northward of Punta Ardita met with a remarkable depression opposite that portion of the coast which lies to the southward of that point, and between that and Punta Marzo." Opposite this depression he discovered an inlet, which he named and is now known as Kelly's inlet, large in size, with great depth of water and well protected. Into this the river Paracuchichi flows. Landing here, Mr.

Kennish and his party began their explorations, endeavoring to reach the Atrato by the shortest route. The course of the streams, west of what is known as the watershed, was pursued, the summit of the mountain crossed at a height of 540 feet, the descent made over a series of falls to the Nerqua river, which was followed to the Truando; thence the party entered the Atrato and thus crossed the isthmus to the Atlantic.

In his report Mr. Kennish proposed the construction of a canal or "new river aqueduct," to flow from the lagoons of the river Atrato into the Pacific, forming an uninterrupted connection with the Atlantic, suitable for the largest ships, and with a current of about two miles an hour. The course, as indicated above, was to be from the mouth of the Atrato on the Atlantic side, to Kelley's inlet, on the peninsula of Paracuchichi, on the Pacific. According to his plans it would be necessary to have a jetty, or line of pilings, on both sides of the entrance to the mouth of the Atrato; from thence to the confluence of the Truando no works would be required, excepting such as were found necessary to prevent the wash of sedimentary particles into the main prison. He also proposed to turn the course of the river Nerqua. But the most conspicuous feature in the plan of Mr. Kennish was that which provided for the construction of a great tunnel, eleven miles and 1630 yards in length, the top to be ninety feet above high water mark.

We have before us the estimate of the cost of the whole work, the amount of which is $150,000,000.*

---

* A summary of the estimate cost of the canal and appurtenances.

Works at the mouth of the Atrato	$ 50,800
Excavations under water in the Truando	1,360,000
Excavations at the confluence of the Truando, including coffer-dams and pumping	40,000
Excavations between confluence, as above, and Pacific (excepting tunnel) the qnanities are all called rock; the excess by these measures being allowed, for grubbing and clearing at $⅞ per cupid yard	77,883,994
Tunnel at $2, being $10 per heading, &c.	25,403,840
Harbor and Kelley's inlet	150,000
Lighthouses	35,000
Piers	20,000

The explorations of the Atrato by Trautwine, Lane and Kennish, attracted such general attention, that Congress appropriated a sum of money to be devoted to a further survey. This led to the expedition of Lieut. (now General) Michler, the result of which corroborated in all respects the previous examinations.

That southern section of the Isthmus, lying between the Panama railway line and the main-land of South America, was recently selected by the Government of the United States for the field of renewed explorations. These investigations have been occasioned by a desire to ascertain if, in consequence of a depression of the Cordilleras in this vicinity, the conditions presented are sufficiently favorable, with or without the use of rivers, to render possible the construction of a ship canal. The expedition arrived at the Isthmus early in February, and is at work at the present time. It is only to be regretted that, in selecting the time of the year, the influence of the climate upon such operations has not been taken into account, as there remains scarcely time enough this year for accomplishing the purposes of the expedition, unless it will be exposed, in continuing its labors beyond the proper time, to the difficulties and dangers of the rainy season.

Depots (Pacific)	50,300
Depots and hospitals on line	35,000
Depot and hospital, Townsend's Junction	15,000
Depot at Turbo and improvements necessary	70,000
Executive department, 12 years	180,000
Engineering department	562,000
Medical department	120,000
Pay department	140,000
Commissary department	260,000
Quartermaster department	150,000
Supplies for ditto	550,000
Twenty-five pumping and hoisting engines for the work in the great cut	1,250,000
Contingencies 25 per cent	27,081,408
	$135,407,042
If the work is estimated at $1, this would be, with contingent allowance, about extra	10,000,000
	$145,407,042

Extract of "*On the junction of the Atlantic and Pacific oceans and the practicability of a ship canal without locks by the valley of the Atrato,*" by Frederick Kelly.

In any event, even if the labors of the expedition are interrupted by the unfavorable season, enough information will, without doubt, be obtained to enable us to form some kind of definite opinion concerning the different projects presented up to the present day for a ship canal upon this part of the Isthmus.*

MODERN ENTERPRISES.

The acquisition of California by the United States, and the commercial activity which resulted from the discovery of the gold fields, so immediately followed by a similar discovery of the precious metal in Australia, the consequent rapid development of trade with the western shores of the North American continent, the extension of commercial enterprise throughout the whole of the Pacific and Indian oceans; all concurred in rendering the realization of the project of an interoceanic communication across the American continent indispensable. Of all the undertakings which have had this object in view, the first, to be brought to a successful conclusion, was that of a railroad from Navy bay, on the Atlantic side, to the city of Panama on the Pacific.

PANAMA RAILROAD.

This project was conceived prior to the year 1849. Work was begun upon it in 1850, and, in five years after, a line of about fifty miles of rail was in active operation.

At the first examination the observer is struck by the fact that a line of communication, evidently created to meet the requirements of our own people, should be situated at a

* At the moment when these pages are sent to the printer, the expedition has returned. No official report has been yet published, but all that we know of the work of the expedition shows clearly that it has not realized its expectation. No favorable locality has been discovered either at Darien, or in the Atrato basin. No project will be proposed for that part of the Isthmus, the cost of construction of which would not exceed the limits, which are naturally fixed for such an enterprise by the relations between the capital involved and the revenue which the use of the work is capable of returning, Let us also add, that no route on the southern part of the Isthmus, if it should even answer the other requirements as to relative cost, would offer such features as would be calculated to awaken the special interest of our people.

distance of more than two thousand miles from its frontiers. This fact becomes the more remarkable, when we consider that the road in question was built to facilitate the relations between the Atlantic and Pacific coasts of the United States. The narrowness of the Isthmus itself at the point chosen for the enterprise, and the consideration of the shortness of the distance to be penetrated, have evidently influenced the promoters of the work out of all due proportion; as if, when the business of shortening the protracted voyage around Cape Horn was in question, it was also necessary to prefer the shortest line for a communication across Central America.

The cost of construction would not have been increased by the selection of a point further to the north. On the other hand, the harbors at the termini of the Panama line are certainly inferior to those which are to be found at a number of other points between the Goatzacoalcos and the main-land of South America, and which would have been much better adapted to the requirements of interoceanic communication. Finally, when we take into account the natural obstacles which opposed themselves to the construction of a railroad at Panama, and the climate of that region, which has cut down so many victims, and whose evil reputation is proverbial, we vainly ask ourselves what could have been the reason for consigning to a distance, of more than two thousand miles from our frontiers, a road from which the United States had so very much to expect.

How often has the traveler groaned over the necessity of descending into the torrid zone on his voyage from the Atlantic coast to our Pacific states. What a length of detour is occasioned by this singular location of the road, what an augmentation of expense to passengers and freight, while a more northerly selection would have been so natural and so easy! Decidedly, our attempts at interoceanic communication have not accomplished a very brilliant *debut*.

The promoters of the Panama railroad pretend that the amount of traffic with California is small, compared with that of the western coast of South America, the commerce of which seems to be one of the principal elements in the prosperity of that concern. We gather, indeed, from the reports of the business transacted in 1860, that fourteen fifteenths of the traffic belonged to countries on the west coast of South America, and that California supplied but one fifteenth; but may we not readily attribute this fact to the unfavorable location of the road itself with relation to the trade between the Atlantic and Pacific coasts of North America? The fact that the railroad is located under the tenth degree of northern latitude presents by no means more advantage for the commerce of South America than if it had been placed ten degrees further north, for, the movement being from northeast to southwest, the only requirement is a southerly passage, it being of no manner of importance whether the ascent or descent be upon the one ocean or the other. In other words, an interoceanic transit offers no better facilities to the traffic of the west coast of South America at 10° than at 20°. To allege the necessities of the commerce of the South, to justify the location of an interoceanic railway at Panama, is nothing more than a geographical heresy.

The enterprise has been, nevertheless, a pecuniary success, for inconvenient as it was, it was the only means of interoceanic communication open to the public, and with all its imperfections it presented such great advantages that its business connections increased day by day. There was, however, a moment when nature asserted her rights, if we may use the expression.

At the time of the great emigration to California, when an unusually large tide of passengers was endeavoring to secure the means of crossing to the western coast, the deficiency became too plainly manifest, and two new routes were opened across more northern parts of the Isthmus, as if to protest against the existing abnormal condition of affairs. A railroad was to have been constructed, at that time, across the isthmus of Tehuantepec, and during the preliminary operations of the enterprise, the management established a mail service from sea to sea. At Nicaragua, steamship transportation had been effected through the river San Juan and the lake to the southern shore of the latter, and thence over land to the Pacific by mule trains. By employing these new routes the public saved time and money.

The temporary pressure passed away; the rush of passengers subsided to the ordinary limits; the enterprise of Tehuantepec, which had for a short time kept the transit open, was abandoned; circumstances of another nature strangled the Nicaragua enterprise; and the Panama returned to the full enjoyment of its privileges. These privileges, like those of all monopolies, when abused, lose continually more and more of their prestige. The high tariff on the Panama railroad and the progress made in steamship navigation have given rise to a steamship line from England to Valparaiso, and to day the Pacific Mail Steam Navigation Company is on the eve of establishing a semi-monthly line of steamers from Panama to Liverpool by way of the straits of Magellan.

The character and geographical position of the country, through which the line of the Panama railroad has been carried, is such as to have called forth the exercise of energies well worthy of a better cause. The first thirteen miles, beginning at Navy bay, were built through a deep morass, covered with the densest jungle, reeking with malaria, and abounding with almost every species of wild beasts, noxious reptiles and venemous insects known in the tropics. Farther on, though some of the land was fair and beautiful, the greater part of the line was through a rugged country, along steep hill-sides, over wild torrents, until the summit-ridge was surmounted, when it descended abruptly to the shores of the Pacific ocean. The entire length of the road was 47 miles and 3000 feet, with a maximum grade of 60 feet to the mile. The summit grade was 258 feet above the assumed grade at the Atlantic.

Commencing at the city of Aspinwall, on Limon or Navy bay, the Atlantic terminus, latitude N. 9° 21′ 22″ and long itude 79° 53′ 52″ W. of Greenwich, the road skirted the western shore of the island of Manzanilla, for about three-quarters of a mile, then bent to the east and crossed the channel which separates the island from the main-land at a point nearly central to the breadth of the island, thence around the southern and eastern shore of Navy bay until it reached the small river Mindee; then it stretched across the peninsula formed by this bay and the river Chagres up to the mouth of the river Obispo, one of its branches, following the course of that river and touching it at intervals of two or three miles. The line continued upon the right or easterly bank of the Chagres as far as Barbacoas (25 miles from Aspinwall), where it crossed the river, and then followed the left bank of the Chagres to the mouth of the Obispo. After striking that river the line followed the valley of this stream to its head in the summit ridge at 10 miles from the Pacific. The summit ridge was passed by a cut one-fourth of a mile in length and twenty-four feet in depth, and then the line struck the head waters of the Rio Grande, which flows into the Pacific ocean. Following the left bank of this river, and descending by a grade of sixty feet to the mile, for the first four miles, the line crossed the rivers Pedro Miguel, Caimitillo and Cardenas; thence it stretched across the savannas of Corrisal and the swamps of Correnden, cut through a spur of Mount Ancon, and reached the Pacific ocean at Playa Prieta, the northern suburbs of the city of Panama.

Some idea of the magnitude of the bridge and culvert work may be obtained when it is known that the water-ways on the route were no less than one hundred and seventy in number, viz: one hundred and fifty-four culverts, drains and bridges ten feet and under, the remaining bridges ranging from twelve to six hundred and twenty-five feet in length. The construction of this railroad has cost $8,000,000.

We here give some statistics relative to its working, those of the year 1860, the last which the Panama Railway Company has made public:

RECEIPTS.

For passengers.....................	$688,378.74
Freight, merchandise (including baggage)............................	618,578.04
Freight, treasure....................	128,946.38
Mail transportation..................	50,000.00
Wharfage, light money &c...........	14,972.66
Earnings uncollected estimated......	50,000.00
Total,....	$1,550,875.82
Running expenses, including materials, repairs, subsistence &c.............	400,050.00

In former years the results were as follows:

	Receipt.	Running expense.	Net profit.
1857.	$1,305,819.	$348,387.	$ 957,432.
1858.	1,506,076.	386,234.	1,119,842.
1859.	1,925,444.	416,818.	1,508,626.
1862.	1,712,281.	483,801.	1,228,480.

During the five years ending in December, 1859, about 196,000 passengers have crossed over the Panama Railway, an average of about 40,000 per annum.

Statement of goods transported over the Panama railroad during the year 1860.*

Going to San Francisco............	Tons	7,667
" Central America...........	"	3,284
" the western coast of South America.........................	"	1,130
Coming from San Francisco, Merchandise....................	"	73
Specie....................	Millions of dollars	38

COMING	Number of Hides.	NUMBER OF PACKAGES OF Coffee	Skins	Indigo	Cochineal	India Rubber	Bark	Balsam	Cocoa	Ores	Copper	Tobacco	Sundries
From Central America	65899	8270	745	5420	6239	777	4	286	5	359		7	132
From the Western Coast of South America	2017		979			188	571		1706		6243	93	52

*From "*Illustrated history of Panama Railroad*," by F. N. Otis.

THE PACIFIC RAILROAD.

It was speedily discovered that the Panama railroad by no means fulfilled all the requirements of an interoceanic transit, particularly with relation to the connection between our own Atlantic and Pacific coasts and our Asiatic commerce, and a deep interest was excited, in consequence, in the construction of a line of rail, with a western terminus at San Francisco, which should be welded, at its eastern end, with the already existing lines from the Atlantic to the Missouri river.

The construction of such a railroad was a work of no ordinary magnitude. The distance from the Atlantic to the Pacific, adopting the existing line of roads between New York and the Missouri, and following from thence very nearly a direct line, is not less than 3,300 miles. In 1863 the western terminus of the railroads built in the direction of the Pacific was at Omaha, Nebraska, 1,402 miles from the Atlantic. From San Francisco a railroad had been built to Sacramento, 117 miles easterly. The gap between these two points has been closed up within the last five years, and, in May of last year, the entire line was opened for use from sea to sea. Comparatively little was done towards the execution of this great enterprise from 1863 to 1865, but during each of the two succeeding years, over three hundred miles were built, and, in 1868, eight hundred miles were laid. Finally, in the latter half of last year, the road was completed.

It required the assistance of the Federal Government to bring about this result, and the aid was furnished in the shape of a loan of government bonds to the companies. The network of roads, to which this loan was made applicable by the Act of Congress, comprised 2,400 miles of rail, to wit: Union Pacific Railroad, 1,053 miles, from Omaha to Ogden, Utah; Central Pacific of California, 747 miles, from Ogden to Sacramento; Kansas Pacific Railroad, Eastern Division, 400 miles; Central Pacific Branch Railroad, 100 miles; Sioux City Branch Railroad, 100. The latter three, forming branches of the main line, are not yet completed.

The government subsidy varies, per mile of road built, in proportion to the assumed cost of construction, and is divided into three classifications; the first, of $16,000 per mile; the second, of $32,000 per mile, and the third, of $48,000 per mile. It follows, from this, that when the auxiliary lines are finished, the government will have loaned its credit to these roads, for the 2,400 miles, to the amount of $63,616,000, as follows:

1,124 miles, at the rate of...............	$16,000.
976 " " "	32.000.
300 " " "	48,000.

The bonds issued by the government for this especial purpose are payable in currency, and bear 6 per cent. interest. They have been delivered to the companies constructing the lines, for them to negotiate, and the government is secured for the reimbursement of the loan by a second mortgage lien upon the roads. The government mortgages are preceded by others of an equal amount, issued by the companies. Independent of these bonds, the companies have received from the Federal Government grants of land of 12,800 acres per mile. This part of the subsidy amounts to about 30,000,000 acres.

From these figures it will be easy to calculate the amount devoted to the construction of the railway line from Omaha to Sacramento;

Union Pacific R. R.....	1,053 miles....	$90,000,000
Central Pacific R. R.....	747 "	60,000,000
	1,800 miles.	$150,000,000

or at the rate of $90,000 per mile for the first and $80,000 per mile for the second. The rapidity with which, in the latter part of the time indicated, the required labor was accomplished, and which rises to almost the dignity of a miracle, might, if necessary, be offered in justification of the excessive amount of these figures in proportion to the topographical difficulties overcome.

The eastern initial point of the main line was fixed in the original act upon the 100th meridian, west from Greenwich, and between the north fork of the Kansas and the northern margin of the valley of the Platte, which was also to be the point of convergence of three branch lines, provided for in the original act: one based upon Sioux City, Iowa, one upon Atchison, Kansas, and one upon Kansas City, Missouri. The line for the eastern part of the route is up the valley of the Platte, which has a course due east from the base of the mountains. Till these are reached, this valley presents probably the finest line ever adopted for such a work for an equal distance. It is not only straight, but its slope is very nearly uniform towards the Missouri, at the rate of about 10 feet to the mile. The soil on the greater part of the line forms an admirable road-bed. The river, after leaving the mountains, has very few affluents, the only bridges constructed for this distance, of about 500 miles, being one over the Loup fork and the North Platte.

The base of the mountains is assumed to be at Cheyenne, 517 miles from the Missouri. This part is elevated 6,062 feet above the sea, and 5,095 feet above Omaha. From Cheyenne to the summit of the mountains, 8,242 feet above the sea, the distance is 32 miles. The grades for reaching the summit do not exceed 80 feet to the mile.

The elevation of the vast plain, from which the Rocky Mountains rise, is so great that these mountains, when they are reached, present no obstacles so formidable as those offered by the Alleghany ranges to several railroads which cross them. On the Baltimore and Ohio road, for example, the mountains are crossed at an elevation of about 2,600 feet above the sea, and with long grades of 116 feet to the mile. The line of the railroad up the eastern slope of the Rocky Mountains is not so difficult as those, upon which several great works have been constructed in the Eastern States.

After crossing the eastern crest of the mountains, the line traverses an elevated table-land of about 400 miles, to the western crest of the mountains, which forms the eastern rim of the Salt Lake basin, and which has an elevation of 7,550 feet above the sea. Upon this elevated table is a succession of extensive plains, which present great facilities for the construction of the railroad. The whole eastern portion of the great Pacific line, known by the name of the Union Pacific Railroad, is a very favorable one, when its immense length is considered. More than one-half of it is practically level, while the mountain ranges are surmounted by grades, not in any case exceeding those now worked upon some of our railroads.

The crossing of the Sierra Nevada Mountains is effected by the western portion of the line, known as the Central Pacific Railroad, at an elevation of 7,042 feet above the level of the sea, within a distance of 105 miles. It is characteristic of all the rivers draining the western slope of the Sierra that they run in deep and tortuous "cañons," impracticable for railroads. It is equally difficult for any line to cross them at right angles. These physical features compelled the engineers to follow the ridges or divides between the rivers. Upon these a favorable line was formed, involving no grade over 116 feet to the mile, and this for about nine and one-half miles.

From the summit of the Sierra, eastward, to the lowest point on the line in the great basin, near the sink of the Humboldt, the descent is 2,995 feet, distributed over 123 miles. The eastern slope of the Sierra is much more gentle than the western. After the valley of the river Truckee is reached, at a distance of about 14 miles from the summit, the average descent is about 30 feet to the mile. There is no loss whatever in any elevation gained—a remarkable feature in a work threading its way for 150 miles through the most formidable mountain barrier on the American continent. From the lowest point in the great basin, which is elevated 4,047 feet above the sea, the line ascends a distance of 300 miles to an elevation of 6,225 feet, at a point a little east of the Humboldt wells. This ascent of 2,178 feet is very uniformly distributed. From this second summit the line descends by pretty uniform gradients 1,905 feet into Salt Lake valley, within a distance of 120 miles. The difference between the lowest point on the line in the valley of the Humboldt, and the lowest point near Salt Lake is only 273 feet. The distance between the two is 420 miles. This remarkable uniformity of the surface offered great facilities for the construction of the road.

To complete this brief description, we give below the distances of the prominent points of the Pacific line, according to recent surveys, and their elevations above the sea level.*

We cannot recount here all that has been expected from this gigantic work. The popularity of the undertaking has been immense; in the first place, on account of the facilities which it would afford to interoceanic traffic, and, secondarily, for the great advantages which it affords to the development of the vast regions of the extreme West, rich as they are in mineral treasures. The public generally had great faith in the beneficent influence, which this great line would exercise upon our relations with the western coast of our continent and the countries which border upon the Pacific. This road was to become the channel of commerce between Europe and Asia, and to make New York the commercial metropolis of the two worlds; but competent men have formed a

---

* Table showing the distances between the prominent points of the Pacific Railroad and their elevations above sea-level between San Francisco and Omaha :

DISTANC'S	STATIONS.	ELEVATIONS ABOVE TIDE.	DISTANCES.	STATIONS.	ELEVATIONS ABOVE TIDE.
—	San Francisco ..		520	Argenta........	4,550
27	Vallejo's Mills ..	121	584	Elko	5,220
79	Stockton........	22	650	Humboldt Wells	5,650
124	Sacramento	56	792	North Point....	
155	Newcastle	930		Salt Lake......	4,290
178	Colfax..........	2,448	819	Promont'ry City	4,943
193	Alta............	3,625	871	Ogden City.....	4,320
216	Cisco	5,711	937	Wasatch Summ.	7,500
229	Summit Sierra Nevada	7,042	994	Fort Bridger ...	7,009
243	Truckee	5,860	1,095	Green River....	6,092
262	State Line......	5,150	1,230	Bridger's Pass.	7,534
278	Reno	4,530	1,334	Laramie	7,175
311	Wadsworth	4,217	1,376	Sherman	8,242
352	Humboldt Lake	4,047	1,399	Cheyenne	6,062
382	Oreana	4,160	1,734	Fort Kearney..	2,128
418	Mill City.......	4,250	1,904	Omaha	968
448	Winnemuca	4,392			

From "*Manual of the Railroads of the United States, for* 1869-70," by Henry V, Poor.

judgment in advance, concerning the value of this new creation, with reference to the programme which it was to fulfill. Here are the calculations which are presented by the promoters of the enterprise in a report, published in 1868, concerning the volume of traffic destined to traverse the continent from one border to the other.

"We have some authentic facts on which to base a fair estimate of the business of the Pacific Railroad, when it is completed, derived from ship ping-lists, insurance companies, railroads, and general information.

		Tons.
Ships going from the Atlantic around Cape Horn......	100	80,000
Steamships connecting at Panama, with California and China..	55	120,000
Overland trains, stages, &c..........................		30,000

Thus we have two hundred and thirty thousand tons carried westward; and experience has shown that in the last few years the returned passengers from California have been nearly as numerous as those going. So also the great mass of gold and silver flows eastward; laterally, there is an importation of wheat from California and goods from China, by the Pacific route. We may fairly assume, therefore, that the trade each way will be about equal. We have, then, 460,000 tons as the actual freight across the continent.

How many passengers have we? We make the following estimate from the average of people:

100 (both ways) Steamships..............................	50,000
200 " Vessels..............................	4,000
Overland (both ways)............................	100,000
Number per annum	154,000

At present prices (averaging half the cost of the steamships), for both passengers and tonnage, we have this result:

154,000 passengers, $100..............................	$15,400,000
460,000 tons, rated at $1 per cubic foot.............	15,640,000
Present cost of transportation..................	$31,040,000

There can be no doubt that the number of passengers will be more than doubled by the completion of the road; so also, the road would take all the very light and valuable goods, which would be greatly increased by *the China trade.* Taking these things into view—estimating passengers at 7½ cents per mile, and goods at $1 per cubic foot—we have

300,000 passengers, at $150 each..................	$45,000,000
300,000 tons, at $34 each..........................	10,200,000
Gross receipts.....................................	$55,200,000

Suppose that the portion accruing to the Union Pacific Railroad is $30,000,000, estimate the running expenses at one-half, and this would leave a net profit of $15,000,000."

To-day, when the Pacific railroad has been in operation over ten months, every one is well aware that this route offers but little assistance to interoceanic transportation. It is sufficient to know the requirements of commerce, to comprehend that the expectations entertained cannot be realized. Commerce seeks those routes which, at the same time, shorten distances and reduce expenditures, and when great distances are under consideration overland transportation is insufficient: water transit alone can offer a solution of the problem. To suppose that the productions of Asia, in their voyage to Europe, would make use of rails for a distance of more than 3,300 miles, was to commit a commercial anachronism and to sin against the laws of trade, which our age has developed.

The cost of railway transportation in the United States is high, compared with other countries, on account, more especially, of the augmented expense attending the operation of railroads. When, for example, we compare the cost of operating railroads in the State of New York, with the corresponding figures of the English lines, we discover the striking fact that the former is one and a half times larger than the latter.*

* Table showing the difference between the working expenses of American and English railroads. (Published by "*The Manual of the Railroads of the United States* 1869–70.")

	Items of cost per train mileage of running trains upon the railroads of New York for 1867.	Items of cost per train mileage of running trains upon the railroads of Great Britain for 1867.
	CENTS.	CENTS.
Maintenance of way, including iron........	49, 50	12, 70
Repairs of engines and materials............	17, 35	6, 45
Repairs of cars..................................	21, 18	6, 74
Cost of fuel	21, 60	3, 42
Wages of enginemen and firemen............	8, 26	3, 00
Local taxes......................................	5, 50	2, 20
All other charges...............................	42, 61	26, 86
	166, 00	61, 37

The lowest railway tariffs in the United States are those of the Eastern States, where the cost of transporting freight is three cents per ton, per mile. The $34, per ton, for freight mentioned in the estimate of the future receipts of the Pacific railroad, correspond to $1\frac{88}{100}$ cts. per ton, per mile, but the tariff put in actual practice, as soon as the road was opened for use, was $199 per ton, and this is 10½ cents per ton, per mile. Supposing, for the present, that the tariff from New York to Omaha be fixed at the lowest rate, or 3 cents per ton, per mile, the cost for this section of the route would be $43.95 per ton, and, adding this sum to the $199, charged for transportation over the Pacific railroad, we have $242.95, currency, (or at $1.35, $179.25 in gold) as the actual cost of transporting a ton of merchandise from ocean to ocean. The tariff of the Panama Railway Company for the transit from New York to San Francisco, was, before the opening of the Pacific railroad, $140 gold, per ton. The difference in favor of the water transit is thus $39.25 per ton. These figures are significant, when we consider that $140 has been fixed by a company in the full enjoyment of privileges amounting to a monopoly, and, on the other hand, that competition will be sure to lower prices. The margin in favor of the water transit and of the isthmian routes is consequently, in reality, more considerable.

The transportation of merchandise over a line of 3,300 miles in length, and the half of which has only one track, cannot be accomplished at a greater average rate than ten miles an hour, including stoppages. This will require fifteen days for the passage from New York to San Francisco. The same transit is made by way of Panama in twenty-two days, roundabout as that trip unnecessarily is. The difference of time between the sea voyage and the overland route does not justify, as we see, the latter in an augmentation of tariff, as compared with the former rates of the Panama Railway Company, of over 16 per cent.

When we come to apply the cost of carrying freight by way of the Pacific railroad, in comparison with the water transit, to the trade between Europe and San Francisco or

Asia, it becomes evident that the transcontinental railway cannot be employed, with a few possible exceptions, and its utility is even more than problematic should we assume a through tariff of three cents per ton, per mile.

Cost of transporting one ton of merchandise, or 40 feet cube, from Liverpool to New York.........	$5.00
From New York to San Francisco, on rails.......	179.25
By way of the Pacific railroad, in 25 or 30 days....	$184.25
From Liverpool to San Francisco, via Panama (tariff of the steamships in connection with the Panama railroad)	
By way of Panama, in 35 days.....................	72.00

From Hong Kong to San Francisco the freight is $20 per ton. When we add to this $184.25, per ton, for freight from San Francisco to Liverpool, by way of the Pacific railroad, we find the total cost amounting to $204.25, from Hong Kong to Liverpool, via the Pacific railroad, in 55 days, whilst the tariff of the Royal Mail Steamship Company, for the same distance is £19.15s 5d, or $98.75, in 60 days.

The difference between the actual tariff of 10½ cents, and that of 3 cents is more than three to one, and we do not believe that the companies controlling the road from Omaha to San Francisco are able to reduce by two-thirds the amount of their receipts. This is the more evident, when we take into consideration the general conditions under which their road is operated, and the sources from which they derive their freight business. If we admit, however, that hereafter it will be possible to put in force the 3ct. tariff, we should obtain then, for the freight from New York to San Francisco $100.59 per ton, instead of $179.25. Difference, $78.66. The freight from Liverpool to San Francisco would thus be reduced to $105.59 against $72. by steamship, in combination with the isthmian transit, and that from Hong Kong to Liverpool would be reduced from $204.25 to $125.59, against $98.75 by the other route.*

Whichever way we turn the question, we find the Pacific railroad insufficient to meet the requirements of commerce between our Atlantic ports, or Europe, and the western shores of North America and the countries on the other side of the Pacific. Let us not say that the Pacific railroad has not fulfilled its promises, let us rather say that too much has been demanded of it, and that it gives what it can.

The Central Pacific Railroad Company, the section from Ogden to Sacramento, announce as the result of their working from the first of May to December 31st, 1869, 8 months, the following figures;

Gross earnings......................	$4,442,652
Expenses of operation..............	2,198,197
Net earnings...................	$2,244,455

*To demonstrate the reduction of the rates upon return freights we insert the following extract from the latest published tariff of the "Compagnie Générale Transatlantique" for the transportation from China, Japan, California, and the western coast of Mexico to Europe in the time which has been above indicated.

DESCRIPTION OF MERCHANDISE.	Tonnage.	From Yokohama, Nagasaki, Shangai, and Hong Kong, to		
		Saint Nazaire.	Paris, Lyons, Marseilles, Havre.	London.
Silk	40 cub. feet	$120,	$128.	$130.
Tea	40 "	69.	77.	79.
General Merchandise	40 " or 2,240 lb.	95.	103.	105.

DESCRIPTION OF MERCHANDISE.	Tonnage.	From San Francisco, to		From Acapulco to	
		Paris, Havre, Bordeaux.	London, Liverpool, Antwerp, Rotterdam, Hamburg.	Paris, Havre, Bordeaux.	London, Liverpool, Antwerp, Rotterdam, Hamburg.
		L. S. D.	L. S. D.	L. S. D.	L. S. D.
Quinine	2,240 lb.	15.	16. 1.	14.	15.
Cochineal	2,240 lb.	19. 5.	20. 11.	18. 10.	19. 10.
Cotton	40 cub. feet	7. 12. 6.	8. 12. 6.	7. 12. 6.	8. 12. 6.
Caoutchouc	2,240 lb.	13. 8.	14. 8.	13. 8.	14. 8.
Sarsaparilla	40 cub. feet	7. 10.	8. 10.	7. 10.	8. 10.
General Merchandise	40 cub. feet or 2,240 lb.	13.	14. 5.	13.	14. 5.

Judging from the details of the receipts for the month of September, which we give below, we should say that the receipts are about equally divided between freight and passengers.*

From the figures above quoted, we may fairly estimate the gross receipts of the Central Pacific Railroad for the whole year at $7,000,000. We have no reports of the receipts and cost of working of the Union Pacific Railroad, the section from Ogden to Omaha, but it is suppossed that the result for that section of the line will be in similar proportion.

It was estimated, in the report to which we have referred, that the receipts of the entire line of the Pacific railroad for through freights would be $55,000,000 of which $30,000,000 would belong to the Union Pacific, and $25,000,000 to the Central. This calculation is therefore evidently illusive, for we have seen that the last section gives for its total receipts only $7,000,000 in which the local traffic is credited with 70 per cent.† leaving but 30 per cent. or something like $2,000,000, where 25,000,000 had been expected! That which good judges had prophesied, is to-day confirmed by experience. The great transcontinental line has not, leaving out passenger transportation, presented to our international traffic any material improvement over the route by steamships in connection with the Panama transit, and is even inferior to it in some respects; unsatisfactory as is the present condition of that passage.

---

* Passengers,		$302,259.29
Sleeping Cars,		11,498.41
		$313,757.70
Freight,	$262,250.32	
Express,	15,704.83	
Mail,	15,248.20	
Wharf,	1,250.95	
Miscel aneous,	1,023.21	
Telegraph,	552.69	
		296,030.20
Total receipt for the month of September, 1869		$609,787.90

† This is the proportion indicated in the circular addressed January 1, 1870, to the bondholders of the Central Pacific Railroad, by Messrs. Fisk & Hatch, New York.

WORKS UNDER CONSTRUCTION.

From all that we have said, it is abundantly evident that the true mission of the Pacific railroad is to develop the resources of the vast regions which it traverses, and to unite them with the other states, rather than to facilitate international commerce; but a tangible advancement is being prepared in the latter direction, and merits especial attention at our hands, as, in any event, it will be, for a long time to come, the best means of facilitating our commercial relations with the western coast of our own continent and the countries beyond the Pacific.

RAILROAD ACROSS THE ISTHMUS OF TEHUANTEPEC.

The enterprise, which has for its object the construction of an interoceanic railroad across this isthmus, has been organized under a concession from the Republic of Mexico, given January 2d, 1869, and there is every appearance that, within a short time, this line will be in the actual performance of those services which the commerce of the world may reasonably expect from it.

To judge from the surveys and plans already made, the line will start from a point near the mouth of the Goatzacoalcos, flowing into the Gulf of Mexico, and runs south, in nearly a direct line, to the foot of the Cordilleras, leaving Minatitlan on the left, and arising by a regular grade to Jaltepec, 110 feet above the level of the sea; the line from thence south following a depression in the ridge and rising for one and a half miles at the rate of 60 feet to the mile, to the summit which divides the waters of the Jaltepec from those of the river Jumuapa. This summit is just south of the Picadura, to Suchil, and is 290 feet above the tide. The line thence descends for 8 miles, crossing several branches of the Jumuapa until it reaches the latter at Paso de la Puerta; crossing the river at this place at a height of 155 feet above tide; the line then follows a branch of the Jumuapa, which lies in the direction of the

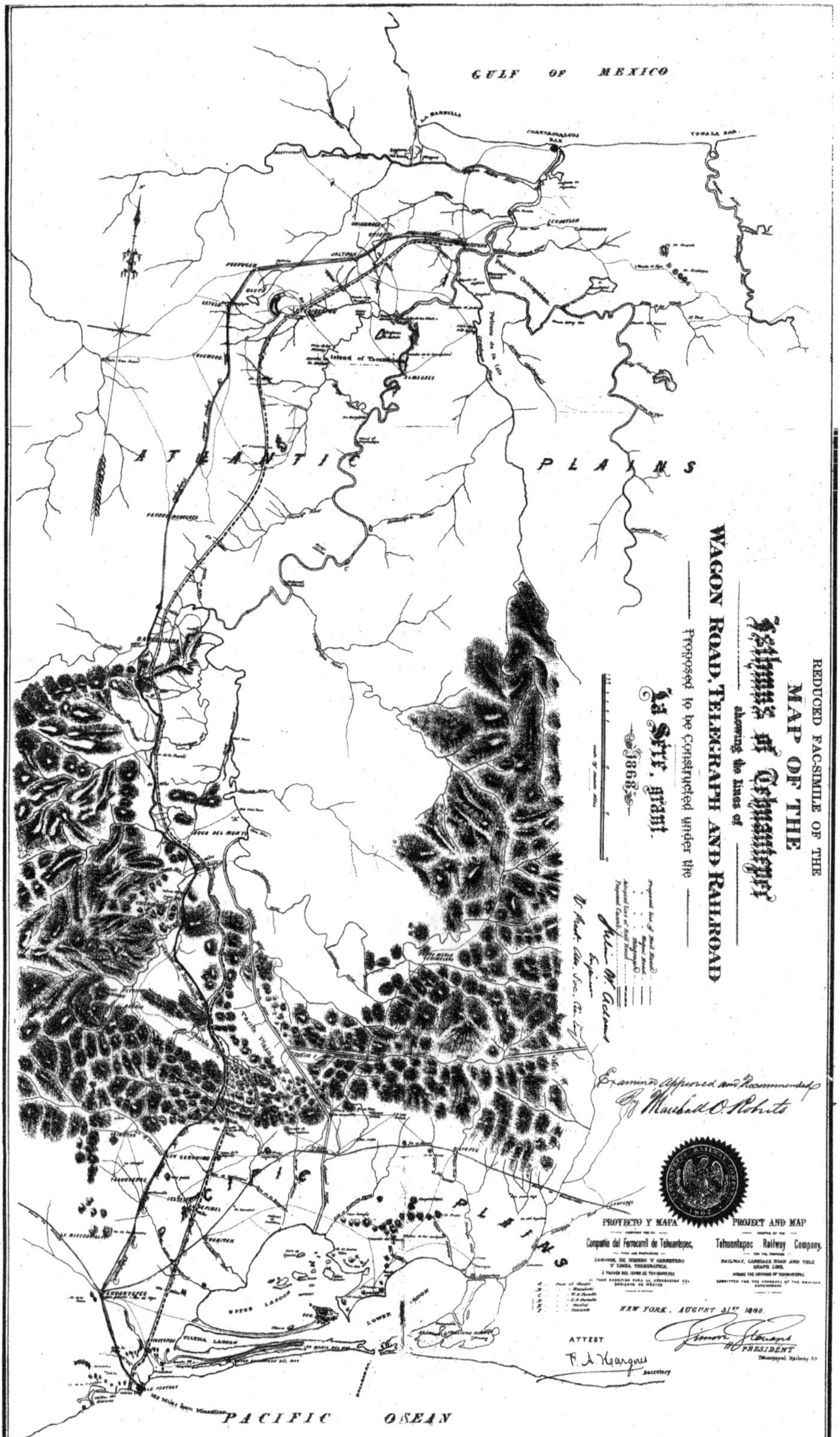

The location of the line of railway, shown upon this map, was revised in May and June, 1870, by a Joint Commission, appointed by the Company and the Government of Mexico, and the new location from Minatitlan to Salina Cruz is indicated thus ------------ . Upon this map is also indicated the line of the proposed Ship Canal.

route to the summit between the valleys of the Jumuapa and the Sarabia, a distance of 6 miles, two miles of which, at the rate of 60 feet to the mile, with a total rise in that distance of 195 feet. From this summit the line continues direct to the Sarabia, a distance of 4 miles, over a gently undulating profile and crossing the latter river at a height above tide of 305 feet (or a fall of but 47 feet in four miles) curves to the eastward and following a branch of the Sarabia for two miles, with a rise of 20 feet per mile, reaches the summit between the Sarabia and Malatengo, at a height above tide of 340 feet; thence following, over a gently descending grade, a tributary of the Malatengo, it crosses the latter river about 280 feet above tide, and near its junction with the Almaloya, and skirting the base of the upland between the two rivers, takes the valley of the Almaloya, which it follows to the plains of Chivela, a distance of 24 miles, rising, in that distance, 410 feet, or a mean rise of 17 feet per mile, with no grade of over 25 feet per mile, still following a branch of the Almaloya, it crosses the Chivela plains, and enters the pass of Masahua at a height of 793 feet above tide, or a rise of 103 feet in 4½ miles. This is the extreme height of the grade at the summit pass which divides the waters which flow into the Pacific from those which flow into the Atlantic.

At this point, within a hundred yards of the head of waters of the Altmaloya, a branch of the Rio Verde, heads up between Cerro Espinosa and Cerro Masahuita of the Masahua range, and offers a means of gradual descent to the Pacific plains.

The harbor by means of which the line will communicate with the Pacific, will be either that of Ventosa or Salina Cruz. The cost of constructing the railway, 162 miles in length, will be in the neighborhood, according to the latest estimates, of $8,000,000—precisely the sum which was expended for the construction of the Panama Railroad. This circumstance is readily explained by the comparatively greater advantages which are presented, in the present instance, by the topographical conformation of the region through which the road is to be built, and by the character of the country itself, which offers those resources for construction purposes, of which the Panama enterprise was deprived.

The point which imperatively commands our attention, at the outset, is the fact that the isthmus of Tehuantepec is situated only 500 miles from the southern frontiers of the United States, and is accessible by means of the Gulf of Mexico, which is destined to become, in fact, an American lake, when, in consequence of the improvement of river navigation, the shipping from our interior commercial centres shall be able to extend their voyages to the coast.

If we look at the map of the American continent, it will be seen that the isthmus of Tehuantepec is the most favorable point at which an interoceanic communication can be established, whether we consider it specially with reference to the United States alone, or to the other American and the European and Asiatic countries. From Europe, or the United States, to the Pacific, it is the shortest route of any either now in operation, or that is at present contemplated, with the exception of the Pacific railway, the restricted utility of which we have already demonstrated with reference to transcontinental transportation. This is exhibited by the following table, showing the respective distance from England, New York and New Orleans, to the port of San Francisco in California, by the routes of Panama and Tehuantepec, compared with the voyages from the same places round Cape Horn, and showing also the distance each would respectively save by traversing the American isthmus:*

Voyage to San Francisco (Cal.)	Round Cape Horn.	Via Panama.	Via Tehuantepec.	Dif. in Favor Tehuantepec.
From.	Stat. Miles.	Stat. Miles.	Stat. Miles.	Stat. Miles.
England (Liverpool)	15,710	8,607	7,476	1,131
New York	16,360	6,218	4,741	1,477
New Orleans	16,500	5,718	3,384	2,334
Saved by		Distance Saved Via Panama.	Distance Saved Via Tehuantepec.	
England		7,163	8,234	1,131
New York		10,142	11,619	1,477
New Orleans		10,782	13,116	2,334

* From "*The Tehuantepec Railway, its location, features and advantages under the La Sere Grant*, 1869."

In order to complete the above table, so far as it concerns our trade with California, we present a comparative detailed table of distance and time for voyages from New York and New Orleans to San Francisco by the two routes, according to the statements of distances (in statute miles) in the "*Memoir on Ocean Routes*," published in 1857, by Cap. F. J. Cram.

The time required in each voyage, as indicated, including the delays rendered necessary by the discharge and reshipment of cargoes, is calculated from the average figures presented by the *log books* of the steamers, connecting with the isthmus of Panama, on the two oceans.

New York to Aspinwall.........	2,392	miles in	8	days.
Aspinwall, by railroad to Panama.	51	" "	1	day.
Panama to San Francisco........	3,775	" "	13	days.
Total for the route of Panama.	6,218	" "	22	"
New York to the Goatzacoalcos..	2,275	" "	8	"
Railroad across the Isthmus......	162	" "	1	day.
Isthmus to San Francisco........	2,304	" "	8	days.
Total for the route of Tehuantepec	4,741	" "	17	"
Difference in favor of Tehuantepec.	1,477	" "	5	"

By adopting for the trip from New York to the Goatzacoalcos the route of Fernandina (Florida),* the distance be-

* The dangerous navigation of the Florida Cape imposes to commerce the highest rates of insurance, from which it is at present proposed to escape by adopting the Fernandina transit for the cotton transportation from New Orleans, Mobile and other gulf ports to New York. It seems, at first, extraordinary that a direct navigation should be supplanted by any combination, especially if involving successive re-shipments; for the cotton of New Orleans and other gulf ports crosses the gulf to Cedar Keys, thence by rail across the peninsula of Florida to Fernandina, where it is again embarked; but all is explained when we consider the freqnency of severe maritime disasters in the vicinity of the cape, and the high premiums demanded by the underwriters. That which has been practiced with success by the commerce between one part of the United States and another, has been found of equally advantageous application in the transportation of the products of the South to Europe, which for the same reason is done for lower freights, when the cotton is taken in charge at Fernandina, than at New Orleans, or at the other ports of the gulf. It will not be astonishing if, before long, Fernandina shall become, as one may say, the very key of the navigation of the Gulf of Mexico, in its connections with Europe and the northern ports of the United States.

comes reduced from 2,275 miles in 8 days, to 2,160 miles in 7 days (according to the tables of distances furnished by the Bureau of Navigation in the Department of the Navy at Washington), as follows:

New York to Fernandina......	969	miles	in $3\frac{1}{2}$	days.
Fernandina, by railroad to Cedar Keys..................	154	"	" 1	"
Cedar Keys to the Goatzacoalcos	1,037	"	" $2\frac{1}{2}$	"
Total	2,160	"	" 7	"

It follows that, taking into account the saving obtained by the Fernandina route, susceptible of augmentation by a more perfect connection between the different lines of transportation, the difference in favor of Tehuantepec is increased from 1,477 miles and five days, to 1,592 miles and six days.

The further south we come in the United States, the more clearly evident become the advantages of the Tehuantepec route. New Orleans is but 918 miles from the mouth of the Goatzacoalcos, and twelve days suffice for the voyage from New Orleans to San Francisco, as follows:

New Orleans to the Goatzacoalcos...	918	miles	in 3	days.
Railroad across the isthmus.........	162	"	" 1	day.
Isthmus to San Francisco...........	2,304	"	" 8	days.
Total	3,384	"	" 12	"
The same trip, via Panama, requires..	5,718	"	" 22	"
Difference in favor of Tehuantepec...	2,334	"	" 10	"

Even supposing, which is not so, the existence of a steamship line from New Orleans, by way of Havana, to Aspinwall, in connection with the departures of the steamers plying between Panama and San Francisco.

Résumé of time of Voyages by the two routes.

	Via Panama.	Via Tehuantepec.	Difference in favor of Tehuantepec.
New York to San Francisco.	22	17	5 days.
New York by Fernandina to San Francisco........		16	6 "
New Orleans by Havana to San Francisco..........	22		
New Orleans to San Francisco....................		12	10 "

We have already seen that the geographical position of the isthmus of Tehuantepec offers for the European trade with California, Japan and China an improvement of 1,131 miles.

Let us now examine the position of the new route with reference to the relations of our Atlantic ports and Europe with the western shore of South America. We find that Tehuantepec is ten degrees to the north of Panama, and that freights, leaving Tehuantepec for the south, would be compelled to traverse the Pacific for the entire distance which separates Tehuantepec from Panama, in order to secure the same relative position as those transported by way of Panama. At first sight, this difference in the voyage to be made, presents an apparent disadvantage, which has, nevertheless, no existence for a very simple reason. Either the freights via Tehuantepec here in question, are bound from the Atlantic ports of the United States and from Europe for the western coast of South America, or they leave the ports of Peru and Chili for the Eastern United States and Europe. In the former case their Atlantic trip would be shortened by all the distance between Tehuantepec and Panama. It is therefore evident that they should run upon the Pacific the same additional distance as they would have run upon the Atlantic, in case they had been going by way of Panama. In the latter case the greater distance to be run on the Pacific in order to reach Tehuantepec, compared with the transit by Panama, is compensated by an equal distance saved on the Atlantic side. The question here, as will be seen, is concerning a commercial movement from north-east to south-west, and from south-west to north-east, to which both of the two interoceanic lines can offer equal facilities.

The time when the Atlantic and Pacific will be united by a ship canal is still distant. Everything goes to show that the realization of such an enterprise, from its very magnitude, will involve considerable delay. We are compelled, therefore, to consider the acquisition of means of transportation across an isthmus, situated the nearest of all to our own frontiers, as essentially useful, and as offering a most desirable improvement in view of the incompleteness of the first attempt at Panama.

All that argues in favor of so important and timely an enterprise interests in the highest degree the entire commercial world, and may be stated here with much *apropos.*

In the opening chapter of this essay, we have expressed our regret that the promoters of the first isthmian railroad attached so much importance to the comparatively small length of line to be established, and that, in consequence, they were induced to locate their road in a geographical position so little adapted to the wants of commerce. A few technical explanations will justify this assertion.

The new interoceanic enterprise which we are considering, though the length of its railway is triple, finds itself very nearly in about the same condition as the Panama railway, concerning the cost of transportation. The length of the Tehuantepec road is to that of the Panama as three is to one. The distance, which passengers and goods would traverse on the Tehuantepec road, will be triple that passed over on the Panama; but it does not follow that the working expenses would be triple.

The operation of a railroad gives rise to both regular and accidental expenditures; the former are fixed and the latter are variable. The fixed expenditures comprise the cost of supervising the roadway, of receiving and delivering freight, keeping up the stations, and finally the expenses of general management. The variable expenses are those which arise from the running of the road, and the amount of which varies in proportion to the business movement, viz: the cost of maintaining the road and the rolling stock; the cost of locomotion, properly so-called, such as payment of enginemen, firemen and other special employees; of fuel, oil, grease, and, in short, all that appertains to the locomotion and varies with it. When it is desired to judge of the cost of working a railroad, or to compare it with that of another line, it is necessary to ascertain the amount of variable expenses for each mile run by the trains; on the other hand the fixed expenses are to be accounted comparatively with the length of the line to which they appertain; thus a suitable criterion will be obtained. Such is the classification of expenses when we treat of a railroad under ordinary conditions of running, but when we come to discuss the cost of working lines of 51 miles and 162 miles, placed under special and exceptional conditions as to their operation, such as those of Panama and Tehuantepec, all the expenses become very nearly fixed, except that of fuel, the same amount of personal labor employed for the maintenance of the road, for repairing the rolling stock, and for locomotion, properly so-called, being always indispensable, particularly in such a country as the isthmus, where skilled labor is not to be readily obtained. The movement over these ismithian lines does not exceed an average of two trains per day, going and coming, running 204 miles over the Panama railway, at the rate of 51 miles for each simple train, and 648 miles for Tehuantepec, at the rate of 162 miles per train. The same number of employees occupied in operating the Panama road would be sufficient for the Tehuantepec, because the daily working of the two lines does not differ more than 444 miles. The wear and tear of the roadway for such an excess would be hardly perceptible. The cost of repairs to the rolling stock would not receive a sensible augmentation for the same reason, and the sole actual expenditure occasioned by the surplus running would be that of fuel, which can be counted for 26 cents, at the rate of 60 lbs. coal at $10 per ton, consumed for every mile run. (The consumption of fuel on the Alsacian railroads, in 1844, by trains affording a fair comparison, was from 8 to 10 kilogrames of coke per kilometer of running distance.) We admit, as an addition to the cost of repairs to the rolling stock, 14 cents per mile for the complimentary daily running of 444 miles, say an annual increase of $22,688, which sum would be amply sufficient for this purpose.

Applying now to the general working of the Tehuantepec road the same expenses incurred by that of Panama, with this particularity that the 444 miles, run daily by the former in excess of the number run by the Panama road, occasion an additional expense of together 40 cents (26 + 14) per mile run, we find that a train passing over the Tehuantepec line costs only $44.40 (162 — 51 = 111 × 40 = 44.40) more than passing over that of Panama. The latter figure, multiplied by the daily four trains, produces the sum of $177.60, which represents the excess of the daily expense of the Tehuantepec road over that of Panama, although the former is three times as long as the latter. The question of difference in the cost of working the two lines is therefore reduced to a matter of minor importance, and it is now sufficiently demonstrated that a railway at Tehuantepec allows as satisfactory rates for conveyance as one at Panama.

It must also be observed that the tariff of transportation of any road, crossing the Isthmus, forms but a small part of the entire cost of carrying cargoes, which employ these roads for short a time. Thus, we see that the cost of transit by rail from Aspinwall to Panama, is but a fifth part of the price of transporting a ton of freight from England to California, and this proportion decreases naturally when we come to consider the transit to Asia. There exists, in fact, a remarkable community of interests between the isthmian railways and the enterprises of navigation, which are destined to operate in connection therewith. The more favorable the conditions under which this navigation may be performed, the more beneficial will be its influence upon the prosperity of the whole line, and more particularly upon that of the railways. The best means of obtaining favorable freights from the steamers which, on the Atlantic and the Pacific, unite for the accomplishment of the interoceanic transit, is to assure to them, at the two termini of the railroad, full cargoes, by the concentration of the elements of traffic upon the isthmus.

Moreover as to this, the isthmus of Tehauntepec is placed in a favorable position. Its railway does not traverse a region of which the condition and the climate preclude the development of agriculture or local commerce. This railroad. will not depend only upon the interoceanic transportation, it possesses local elements of freight revenue. The fertility of the isthmus of Tehuantepec and its vegetable and mineral wealth are proverbial. This fact is attested by the reports of the scientific commission, which explored the isthmus in 1852, an extract from which will be found in a volume upon the subject of the Tehuantepec railway, full of interesting and valuable information, prepared with a high degree of good taste, and recently published at New York, by Hon. Simon Stevens, President of the Tehuantepec Railway Company. It is further confirmed by the work published by Mr. Carlos Butterfield, in 1861, on "*Commerce, Trade and Postal facilities between the United States and Mexico.*"

The construction of the railroad across the isthmus, today, will attract foreign capital and colonization, and it is not to be doubted that the face of the whole country of Tehuantepec will be changed, and that agricultural and other industries will avail themselves of all the wonderful natural advantages of this region. This development, which will at first become perceptible along the line of the railroad, will afterwards extend itself, step by step, to the neighboring states which already export. Chiapas and Oaxaca will direct their products towards the isthmus. Tabasco, although it has its own navigation, will come to the Goatzacoalcos to meet an easier market. The principal benefit which will result from the increase of exportation and from the general development of the country will be the additional stimulus given to steam navigation, connected with the ports of the isthmus, and the freight for interoceanic traffic will undoubtedly be favorably affected by such a state of affairs.

RAILROADS ACROSS THE ISTHMUSES OF HONDURAS AND COSTA RICA.

Upon each of these isthmuses there is a railroad in course of construction, but their creation must be regarded as of more importance to the development of the regions through which they run, than to the question of interoceanic transportation. The work, moreover, advances but slowly. These two isthmuses, situated between Tehuantepec on the one hand, and Panama on the other, do not find themselves favorably situated with reference to interoceanic traffic. That of Honduras, situated about 500 miles south of Tehuantepec, cannot present equal advantages with the latter. That of Costa Rica,* about 200 miles north of Panama, is

---

* In a publication made about ten months since, we have remarked as follows, concerning the railway through Costa Rica:

"We have just learned, by an article in the *Panama Star*, that the concession for the establishment of interoceanic communication, accorded in January last by the government of Costa Rica, one of the republics of Central America, has been approved by Congress. It provides for the construction of a railroad 140 miles in length, from Limon, on the Atlantic coast, to the gulf of Fonseca on the Pacific. The republic of Costa Rica has given a subsidy, in favor of the grantees, of its bonds at the rate of $60,000 for each mile of railroad constructed, or of $8,400,000, payable in forty years, and bearing interest at 8 per centum per annum.

"This enterprise does not offer greater probabilities of success than other combinations which have lately been made in Costa Riea. One essential and indispensable condition for the favorable reception of an interoceanie railroad by the public, is that it shall avoid the signal disadvantages of the Panama line, and the geographical position of the Costa Rica line is such as will not permit it to fulfill that condition. The Costa Rica railroad will be placed between those of Panama and Tehuantepec, powerless to supply the deficiencies of the one and unable to sustain a comparison with the other—a position which condemns it to failure in advance. Moreover, with such prospects in view, it will not be able to realize the necessary funds, and it is certain that the endorsement of the government of Costa Rica, a country of three hundred thousand inhabitants and without exceptional resources, will hardly attract the confidence of capitalists to an enterprise so singularly conceived."

not able, for strong reasons, to offer those conditions which American commerce demands of an interoceanic line situated south of the United States.

For this reason, and that we may not exceed the limits assigned to this essay, we will not attempt any further discussion of these two routes.

The predictions which we made at that time have been signally realized, because as we have been given to understand, the contract made for the construction of this road, on the 8th of June last, has been declared null and void by reason of non-compliance with the preliminary stipulations.

CHAPTER SECOND.

The Suez Canal and the Proposed American Ship Canal.

THE SUEZ CANAL.

The configuration of the solid land of this globe of ours, surrounded as it is by water, presents in both hemispheres and in nearly corresponding latitudes, a contraction of the continents to a narrow belt of "isthmus." The old worid isthmus connects Asia with Africa, with a length of but a hundred miles, while that of the new world is made up of the whole central section of the American continent, with an extent of over fifteen hundred miles, from the south of Mexico to the main-land of South America, and varies in breadth from fifty to two hundred miles. The former constitutes a barrier between the Indian ocean and the Mediterranean, compelling the commerce of Europe and Asia to double the cape of Good Hope, the extreme southern point of Africa. The latter is washed on the one coast by the Atlantic, and on the other by the Pacific, and prevents water communication between the opposite shores of the American continent, except by way of the voyage around Cape Horn, and forces this detour alike upon the commerce of the eastern shores of America, and that of western Europe, with Asia.

The isthmus of the old world, the isthmus of Suez, has lately been penetrated, by the energy, perseverance and genius of M. Ferdinand de Lesseps, and a ship canal, of great width and without locks, has been open for use since November last. This is one of the greatest works of the age, already so rich in marvels, and the mind is bewildered in contemplating the probable consequences which will result to the commercial world and the destinies of the human race.

EARLY UNDERTAKINGS UPON THE ISTHMUS.

To judge by the geological formation of the isthmus of Suez, one would be inclined to think that the time has been, when Asia and Africa were separated by a narrow strait, afterwards filled up by the operation of natural causes.*

The isthmus is almost level with the adjoining seas, having a general depression to the Mediterranean. Its average elevation is from five to eight feet above the sea level and, although in the case of two hillocks, it rises to heights of thirty to forty feet. Several salt lakes and swamps exist in the depressed portions.

It has long been an object to the rulers of the adjacent territory to establish a water communication from the Mediterranean to the Red sea, connecting with the Indian ocean. It has been frequently attempted, and more than once with success. Some historians, among them Strabo, attribute the earliest attempt to Sesostris, before the siege of Troy. He adds, however, that it is attributed by Herodotus to Pharaoh Necho, son of Psammiticus, the same who caused Africa to be circumnavigated by the Phœnicians. The entire work was probably not completed until the times of the Ptolemies.

The ancient Egyptian canal did not pass in a line across the isthmus, as in the present case. They sailed on the Nile so far as it was possible, then they excavated a canal with

---

* The engineer Lepere, commissioned by General Bonaparte to explore the line of a Canal upon the isthmus, gave the additional reason, among others, for his belief that once the two seas were one. He said that among all the hieroglyphics of Thebes, there was no trace of anything to show the existence of that useful animal of the East, the camel, even among very many hieroglyphics of inferior animals. Hence he believed that the camel came from Asia into Africa, after the formation of the isthmus.

This indication is noted in a recent publication upon the subject of the Suez Canal, by Prof. J. E. Nourse, to which we are indebted for this and other items of information.

the direct simplicity which was at that time necessary to the execution of such a work, filling it with water of the river which flowed at first northward to lake Timsah, and thence southward through the Bitter lakes to the Red sea, near Suez. This line, as is shown by the vestiges, employing the lakes existing upon the isthmus, just as does the modern canal now built, had four sections, 92 miles in total length, i. e., 13 miles from Suez to the Bitter lakes, 27 miles through these lakes, 40 miles from the lakes to El Ouady, and 12 miles from there to Bubastis, then one of the principal branches of the Nile. Herodotus stated that this canal was four days' journey in length and of a width sufficient to admit the passage of two triremes abreast. The Ptolemies kept the canal in constant repair and added considerable improvements to the great work. Strabo, who traveled in Egypt fifty years before the Christian era, beheld this canal covered with ships. The Roman emperors Trajan, and Adrian especially, greatly enlarged the canal (the vestiges show a breadth of 100 to 200 feet). When the Mussulmans effected the conquest of Egypt, the canal had been abandoned, but the Caliphs, comprehending how necessary it was to renew the work in the interest of the holy cities of Mecca and Medina, soon caused its reconstruction. At the time Mohammed Ben Hassan, having revolted in the city of the Prophet (Medina) against Abon Djafar, then Caliph of Irak, the latter sent orders to his lieutenant in Egypt directing him to fill up the canal, that it might not be used for the transportation of provisions to the insurgents in Medina. His order was carried out, and communication stopped with the Sea of Kolsom (the Red sea). This was in 839 of the Mussulman hegira (1435 A.C.). Since that time water communication between Egypt and the Red sea has ceased.

Antiquity created the Red sea route, the middle age that of the cape of Good Hope and Cape Horn; subsequent centuries have gradually developed the idea of the Grand Canal across Suez. "Every great man," says Thiers, "who looked at the map of the world, has thought of Egypt." It did not fail to occupy the mind of Napoleon, who, in writing to the Directory about the project of uniting the Mediterranean with the Red sea, says, "Alors la Méditerranée deviendra un lac français." When this successor of Alexander arrived in Egypt, he hastened to Suez to determine whether he could recommence the work of the Pharaohs. He tracked the vestiges of the ancient canal upwards of five leagues and went down to the Red sea. He ordered one of the most able engineers of that age, M. Lepere, to examine the question of interoceanic communication, and this engineer became the author of a project for connecting the two seas by way of the Nile; which was simply the reconstruction of the ancient canal. The cost of construction was estimated at 30,000,000 francs. M. Lepere thought of making a "thorough cut" at the point afterwards selected by M. Lesseps, but difficulties in the way of its execution, of various kinds, appeared insurmountable. At that time the prevailing ideas of the relative levels of the two seas were also very erroneous. After the return of the expedition to Egypt, M. Lepere presented to Napoleon a memoir upon the subject of the canal, but he, preoccupied as he was at that time with the events which were preparing his extraordinary career, replied to him: "Eh bien, la chose est grande; publiez un Mémoire et le gouvernement turc trouvera peut-etre un jour sa conservation et sa gloire dans l'execution de ce projet." This remarkable saying has been realized, as, half a century afterwards, the Viceroy of Egypt offered to M. Lesseps the means of prosecuting the enterprise.

When Mohammed Ali became master of Egypt he was inspired with the old ideas. He built the canal of Mahmoud Eeyeh, from Alexandria to Cairo, thus restoring a water communication which had been lost ever since the days of the glory of Memphis. But this line possessed only a local importance, and afforded no aid to the interoceanic transit, the necessity for which began to be felt now that England, during the prolonged peace, had so largely extended her East Indian possessions and her commerce with the Orient.

England never really desired the construction of a canal across the isthmus of Suez, finding her own interests well served by the existing conditions of her East Indian trade. These conditions, by reason of the huge machinery required by that trade, and which she possessed, gave to her merchants a practical monopoly. The cape route was convenient for them. That which England required was only a readier means of correspondence with the Indies; but, even in this direction, she made only an indecisive movement, always actuated by the fear of opening to others the road to India, and of destroying the prestige which she had secured in the East through the difficulties of access of which she had availed herself. In 1840, a steamship service was established upon the two seas, on either side of the isthmus of Suez, completing, by means of mule and camel transportation overland from Alexandria to Suez, the necessary facilities for effecting prompter communication between England and Bombay, Calcutta and China. Only ten years later, the transit across the isthmus was rendered more rapid and easy and still further adapted to the demands of commerce by the construction of a railway, two hundred and forty miles in length, from Alexandria to Cairo, and thence to Suez. This, however, was only a temporary expedient.

THE SHIP CANAL FROM SEA TO SEA.

In 1854, M. Ferdinand de Lesseps presented for the first time a project for an interoceanic ship canal, from the very shore of the Mediterranean, directly across the Isthmus by way of the lakes, to Suez. This project proposed the excavation of a canal ninety miles in length, three hundred and thirty feet wide at the water line, with a gradual slope at the sides to the bottom, which was to be twenty feet below the mean sea level.

In M. Lepere's report the opinion was expressed that the Red sea was thirty feet higher than the Mediterranean. There were to be in consequence, at each end, sluice locks 330 feet long by 70 feet wide. By using the tides, it was hoped that an additional depth of three to four feet might be gained.

At that time the problem of the sea levels had not yet been thoroughly resolved, and it was not until 1847 that the fact was established that no difference of elevation existed. Science is indebted for this important discovery to M. Bourdaloue, well known for his consummate ability in such undertakings, and also to M. Linant Bey, engineer in chief to the Viceroy of Egypt.

If we turn our eyes to our own continent, we find that the same incertitude existed for a long time with reference to the relative levels of the seas which wash the eastern and western shores of America. Nearly forty years ago, Col. Lloyd, examining the American shores both ways between Panama and Chagres, reported the Pacific to be three and a half feet higher than the Atlantic. Col. Childs, who made a survey of the Nicaragua route, fixed the difference of level at only 19 inches. Col. Totten, the engineer of the Panama railroad, had more recently found the greatest difference to be 14 inches; and in some instances it was reported to be only 4 or 5 inches. It therefore became a question whether, in point of fact, the Pacific was at a higher level than the Atlantic, and at the present day it is admitted that the level of the ocean is substantially the same at all parts of the globe, as a consequence of the law of gravitation, and would be so, as long as a pound of sea water everywhere occupied the same space and was composed of the same constituents. When surveys showed different results, it was because the mean tide level had not been ascertained with sufficient accuracy.

The Viceroy of Egypt, in the same year, 1854, accorded to M. Lesseps a concession for the construction of the projected canal; but the necessity of submitting this grant for the sanction of the Supreme Porte, and the Sultan having refused his approval, led to the substitution of another, dated in 1856, upon which the enterprise was finally based.

During the interval between the first and second concessions, the conception of the ship canal had acquired general popularity, in spite of the opposition with which the efforts of M. Lesseps were met on the part of England. In 1855 the project received the approval of an international commission, composed of civil and naval engineers, hydrographical officers of the marine, and others from countries which would be chiefly interested in the work. France, England, Spain, Austria, Prussia, Italy and Holland sent some of their ablest men with M. Lesseps to Egypt, and, after a full investigation of the matter, the plan for navigation in a line from sea to sea was adopted. The report of the commission assured the Viceroy of the practicability of the plan, with a cost estimated to probably not exceed two hundred millions of francs, and represented that "the excavation of the canal was easy, and its success certain, and that the two harbors, requiring construction, presented no extraordinary difficulties."

The following are substantially the terms of the Egyptian concession: The Egyptian government to have the right of selecting the managing director from the largest stockholders, if possible; the concession to last 99 years from the opening of navigation; the works to be at the expense of the company, the Egyptian government conceding public lands to defray the expenses of the undertaking. The government to receive annually 15 per cent. of the earnings, without reference to the dividend or interest to be derived from their stocks. The remainder of the profits are to be divided; 75 per cent. for the general stockholders and 10 per cent. for the original founders; the tariff (to be regulated by the Egyptian government and the company) to be the same for all nations; the company is to have the right of importing tools, machinery, and supplies for the workmen, free of duty. The Viceroy guaranteed the canal to be perpetually *free neutralized* to all merchant vessels, without any distinction of nationality, in their conformity only with the rules of navigation to be established by the company; at the termination of the concession the Egyptian government is to be established in lieu of the company, paying, at a fair valuation, for all the material and appliances in use by the company. But if the company should renew the concession for further successive periods of 99 years, the prepayment of 15 per cent. from the net profit yearly, would be increased 25, 30 or 45 per cent. for such successive periods of their renewed charter. Finally, to recompense the company for their labors and charges, they were to establish and collect the tolls, pilotage, towage, &c., on the canal. The cost of the transit through the canal was fixed at 10 francs per ton of freight, and 10 francs for each passenger.

Subsequently (in 1856), it was provided that four-fifths at least of the workmen should, in all cases, be Egyptians. These native workmen, or *fellahs*, numbered 20,000. The stipulation for their pay was that the mean of their salaries would be two-thirds that was paid in Europe for the same work, and that this mean would be more than one-third above what these *fellahs* had received, up to that time, for work in their own country. They were also to have provided for them healthful houses, good provisions and medical assistance, and, if in hospital, they would receive half pay.

The work of organizing the enterprise progressed until 1858, when, notwithstanding the formidable opposition of England at Constantinople, the formation of the "*Compagnie Universelle du Canal Maritime de Suez*" became a fact, constituted with a capital of two hundred millions of francs ($40,000,000), represented by 400,000 shares. The stock was through M. Lesseps' popularity and energy, supported by the influence of fifty Chambers of Commerce, taken up principally in France, and partly in Austria, Spain, Germany and Italy, in less than two months. The Viceroy had taken thirty millions of the stock of the company. The chartered capital was afterwards increased by a loan of a hundred millions of francs.

The necessary funds having been obtained for commencing operations, the opening of the work was inaugurated in 1859. The canal had been opened for use during the past year, and thus it will be seen that ten years were consumed in its construction. This time would have been very much reduced but for impediments of many kinds, which have arisen to obstruct the enterprise, over all of which M.

Ferd. de Lesseps has been finally victorious. This constitutes one of his principal titles to the glory of having accomplished this grand achievment.

The work was begun without the apparent sanction of the Porte, but the French interests embarked had induced the French government to direct its representatives at Constantinople and Alexandria, to give it every legitimate protection. The enterprise was vigorously prosecuted, and, in May, 1861, when a force of eight thousand laborers was employed, the entire expense had reached about twenty-five millions of dollars—more than half of the capital originally provided for the enterprise. This great expenditure represented the immense supplies required for the labor employed, the cost of the dredging machines, work-shops, &c., &c. By May, 1862, it was expected the waters would soon meet in lake Timsah. About twenty thousand laborers were employed at that time, when, in January, 1863, the death of the Viceroy Mohammed Said, the protector of the canal, gave rise to difficulties which caused a new delay in the execution of the work.

The Sultan, at that time, visited the works personally, and, on his return to Constantinople, published an order forbidding the forced employment of the fellahs, and further disagreeing to the land concessions made by Said Pacha. M. Lesseps protested against this interference, whereupon Ismail Pacha, the successor of Mohammed Said, sent to Paris Nubar Pacha to lay the matter before the Direction of the canal company. They refused to agree to his demands. Nubar Pacha then referred the matter to eminent French jurists. These recommended the company to abandon their extraordinary demands, and to be satisfied with the terms offered by the Sublime Porte, amended some time later.

The works were delayed in their progress in consequence of this dispute, although large numbers of fellahs engaged voluntarily in the work, attracted by the good wages and comfortable quarters of the workmen. The dispute having been referred to the Emperor of the French, he decided as follows: 1. That the concessions of November,

1854, and January, 1856, had the form of contracts mutually binding on each party. 2. That as by the withdrawal of the fellah labor the cost of the work would be increased, the Viceroy should pay an indemnity of thirty-eight millions of francs on that account. 3. That the company should cede to the Viceroy their fresh water canal; that the Viceroy should pay ten millions, representing the cost of construction of that canal, and six millions for the tolls, which the company thereby relinquished. 4. That the company should only retain such lands along the line of the maritime canal as might be necessary for the care and maintenance of the said canal. 5. That the company should cede to the Viceroy their title to all lands capable of cultivation by means of irrigation from the fresh water canal, and for which the Viceroy should pay thirty millions. This last grant made the total indemnification 84,000,000 francs.

It is observed that in the above figures a part of the indemnification is applicable to a "fresh water canal." Preliminary to the works on the isthmus, were the providing of efficient arrangements for a plentiful supply of fresh water in the desert, which was but an extent of saline marshes and a sandy waste, all treeless and trackless. When the excavations first commenced, water had to be conveyed long distances, on the backs of camels, horses and donkeys in leather mushoks and goatskins, and then deposited at intervals on the line of works in small iron tanks; also, all provisions for the laborers, tools and every description of articles required for the works, had to be conveyed in the same manner at great expense. To accelerate the transportation of the necessities the sweet water canal, already mentioned, was rapidly pushed forward to its completion which took place in 1861. This canal was ninety-three and a half miles in length; its width varied from fifty to sixty feet at the water level with a depth of about nine feet. It runs from Zagazig (ancient Bubastis) along the canal formerly constructed by Pharoah Necho, which had been reopened as far as Gazazine, a length of 29 miles, by Mohammed Ali. After leaving Gazazine, the canal runs towards lake Timsah, through the desert which is thereby fertilized. From Timsah, which is now known as Ismaila, the auxiliary canal continues along the western edge of the basin of the Bitter lakes, and thence, approaching the foot of the Geneffe mountains, to the port of Suez, so as to permit the barges and dredges to proceed to the Suez roadstead.

It was by this canal that on the 15th of August, 1865, the first vessel from the Mediterranean by way of the ship canal—at that time terminating at lake Timsah—continued from Ismaila its voyage to the Red sea. By this means a special service was, at that time, organized by the Canal Company for a preliminary transit from one sea to the other, with a view to prepare commerce for the employment of this novel maritime channel. According to the report made by M. Ferd. de Lesseps to the General Assembly of shareholders, on the 2d of August, 1869, the traffic by this route had already become very satisfactory. In 1867 there had been transported across the isthmus 31,281 tons of shipping, and, in 1868, 92,642 tons. The number of passengers in the latter year was 38,227.*

Since the arbitration of the Emperor of the French, the history of the construction of the Suez canal is one of continual progress. On the other hand, the moment the ship canal employing the "fresh water canal," as an auxiliary, admitted traffic, the conveyance of goods and passengers commenced and went forward satisfactorily. The works

* From June 1st 1867, to April 5th 1868, ten months, the entries at Port Said were 1,000 ships, with a tonnage of 232,072 tons. The movement of the preceding year had been but 880 ships, with a tonnage of 146,107. In 1868–'69, the increase was proportionally very large ; it shows, from April 15th 1868, to June 30th 1869, 1,362 vessels, with 637,441 tons. The average daily entrance at Port Said was in :

1866,	406 Tons.
1867,	725 "
1868–'9	1,445 "

It is of special interest to note that at Port Said, and also in the other principal ports, steam vessels become more and more the masters of the new commercial movement. The 637,441 tons, entered at Port Said in 1869, are divided as follows :

Sailing vessels,	334,716 Tons.
Steam "	302,725 "
Total,	637,441 Tons.

(Extract from the *Report of M. F'd de Lesseps, in the name of the Council of Administration, to the Assembly General of Shareholders, August 2d*, 1869.)

were pushed on with fresh energy, and with multiplied mechanical appliances, till, finally, in November last, the canal was sufficiently advanced to admit of navigation from sea to sea.

We are all aware that the termini of the canal are at Port Said, on the Mediterranean, near the ruins of ancient Pelusium, situated in latitude north, 31° 3′ 37″, and at Port Suez, upon the Red sea, 29° 58′ 37″ longitude W. of Greenwich. The maritime canal joins these ports by a line which, for a considerable distance, runs nearly due south. Its length is a little more than 160 Kilometers (99 miles). It has an average width of 328 feet; the width at the base is 246 feet, and the depth of water 26 feet. The ocean screw steamships are about 45 feet in the beam; and our large paddle-wheel steamships 85 feet at the widest. Most large English vessels draw about 24 to 25 feet of water, but the tendency is now in favor of vessels of less draught.

The canal passes through four large natural lakes. The largest of these is called *Lac Amer,* or the Bitter lake, and is situated some ten miles from Suez. The other lakes are Lake Timsah, Lake Ballah, and Lake Menzalleh. Lake Timsah is the smallest of these, and has been drying up for a a long time. These lakes are but ten or fifteen miles distant from each other. The work consisted in deepening the channel through these lakes, cutting a passage through the intervening sections, and building the harbors at Port Said and Suez. The land was principlly sandy, with occasional strata of calcareous blue slate. The difference of level, even at the highest calculation, is only four inches in the mile, so that the current will not be great. Whatever current there will be, will be broken by the lakes.

The divisions of the canal are four in number: that of Port Said, or lake Menzalleh, El Guisr, Ismaila and Suez.

Port Said is 124 miles north of Alexandria, and 30 miles of Damietta. The harbor is artificial; there are two jetties, the eastern and the western. The length of the western jetty is 2500 meters, or nearly 1¾ miles, and that of the eastern 1900 meters. These immense seawalls are constructed from cement blocks made on the spot. The blocks, each weighing 22 tons, with a dimension of about 12 cubic yards, are composed from ⅔ sand and ⅓ hydraulic lime from the quarries of the Theil, situated upon the shores of the Rhone. This is the same process which has been employed for the construction of jetties at Algiers and Cherbourg. The area of the harbor is 51 hectares (120 acres), and the width of its mouth is 400 meters (1300 feet). The work extending from Port Said to Kilometre, one, a distance of 14 miles, has been very important; it passes through a large lake very much subject to the action of the wind and sea, from which it is separated but by a narrow strip of land. The amount of matter excavated here would be represented by 11, 141, 622 cubic metres.

El Guisr is the longest division of the canal, extending over thirty-five miles. As far as El Kantara it is very straight, but after that locality is passed the work is heavy, especially at El Guisr. The cuttings in this neighborhood are the deepest. El Kantara is the principal town of this division. It is twenty-eight miles from Port Said. Lake Ballah is eight miles south of El Kantara. In this neighborhood is the village of El Guisr, which is the highest elevation on the isthmus. The work here was very seveee.

Ismaila, on lake Timsah, owes its origin to the canal. The original canal from the Damietta branch of the Nile extended to the town of Zagazig, fifty miles west of Ismaila. One of the first acts of the present company was to bring it within a few miles of the site of Ismaila. The division of Ismaila is the third. It extends through lake Timsah and the Bitter lakes to Kilometre, one hundred and fifteen.

Suez is the fourth division. The principal operations here consisted: first, in constructing a mole 850 yards in length at the mouth of the canal, to serve as a protection against southerly gales, and against the action of the tide at high water; secondly, in dredging the channel leading from the canal to the anchorage in the roads of Suez; thirdly, in filling up a certain extent of land upon the shore, by means of the dredgings from the channel in the roads of Suez. The mole, which projects from the Asiatic shore, has been constructed with a kind of calcareous rock, quarried on the western shore of the bay. Embankments faced with the same kind of stone, that has been used for the mole, were first built, and afterwards the dredgings were lodged behind the retaining embankment. This process was continued till a considerable elevation above the sea level was obtained. Much land of great value was thus reclaimed and built up.

Dredging machines of every description were employed for the works at the two ports and for the canal generally, through the lakes, and through the level on the long depression southward. In the deep cuttings at El Guisr, varying from 60 to 79 feet, and in the hard stony formation at Chalouf, the work has been done chiefly dry and by manual labor. The greater part of the excavation was accomplished by piece-work. The engineers measured the quantity of earth to be removed, and named the price that would be paid for the work. All requisite implements were provided by the company. The price was such as enabled the laborer to earn from two to three francs, (40 to 60 cents) a day. Owing to the hard and stony formation at Chalouf, it was decided that the work should be carried on dry, and it was fortunate that this course was adopted, because at a considerable depth a stratum of conglomerate rock was found, which would have caused great expense and trouble to remove, had water been admitted. The whole amount of about 52,000 cubic yards was in this section easily blasted and cleared away by manual labor.* This latter information

* Table, showing the variation from the full width, to the reduced width of the Canal.

	LENGTH.
Lakes Menzalleh and Ballah, full width,	38 Miles.
Cutting of El Guisr, reduced width of 190 feet,	9 "
Lake Timsah, full width,	5 "
Cutting of Serapium, reduced,	6 "
Entrance to Bitter lakes, full,	2 "
Bitter lakes, width undetermined,	25 "
Cutting of Chalouf, reduced width,	3 "
Plain of Suez, full width,	12 "
Total	100 miles.
Length of the Canal in full width,	82 miles.
" " " in reduced width,	18 "
Total	100 miles.

is taken from the pamphlet, recently published by Professor J. E. Nourse on the canal of Suez, and which contains some very interesting data.

In order to form an idea of the magnitude of the work, it needs only to be said that the excavation for the canal and ports amounted to seventy-five millions of cubic meters, or about one hundred millions of cubic yards, which had been either transported to the lands adjacent or submerged in the sea.

It appears, from the Balance-sheet of the accounts of the company, June 30th, 1869, which we annex hereunto for a more detailed examination,* that at that time the cost of the

---

* The following is the General Balance-sheet of the Suez Canal Company, exhibiting the whole indebtedness incurred in the construction of the work, and the funds which have accrued from various sources; dated June 30, 1869:

Dr.	*Francs.*
Expenses of organization from 1854 to 1859	2,991,435 27
Construction of general offices	920,310.42
Furniture and material of offices in Alexandria and the administration in Paris	141,266.34
Interest on shares 1859-'69	64,054,393.30
Interest on bonds 1868-'69	7,868,493.75
Extinction of obligations 1868-'69	1,730,000.00
Expenses incurred in contracting loan of one hundred million of francs.	1,436,745.40
General expenses of the administration of the affairs of the company, commissions to agents, and negotiations in France and Egypt, from January 1, 1859, to date	16,961,241.73
Expenses of health department, 1868-'69	607,056.16
Expenses of telegraphs, 1868-'69	145,037.40
Expenses of domain, 1869	17,503.95
Expenses of transportation 1866-'69, including floating and rolling stock, buildings, sheds, and also victualling	8,104,681.23
General expenses of construction advances to contractors on material and victualling	17,213,943.88
Other stores, buildings, &c.	38,341,980.82
Works in the construction of the canal and ports	217,671,670.72
Various running accounts with contractors	6,962,499.46
Running accounts of various services—	
Superior agency in Egypt	14,117,553.88
General direction of works	1,972,250.69
Transit service	3,054,987.15
Telegraph service	492.76
Health department	59,833.72
Capital account—	
Egyptian government on account of grants	30,000,000.00
Balance to be recovered on bonds, for calls fallen due	91,325.00
Various debtors	239,131.85
Cash box and portfolio of the superior agency in Egypt	4,024,000.00
Cash	88,291.08
Bank of France	119,786.71
Agricultural credit	15,095.25
Commercial and industrial credit	4,250,000.00
Société Générale	5,680.28
Société des depots et comptes courants	85,724.45
Securities	524,783.93
Portefeuille (various)	7,839,464.52
Total	451,656,661.10

enterprise amounted to $79,000,000, of which $64,000,000 were for the works and expenses of all kinds, arising from the prosecution of the undertaking from its very beginning, such as material, construction, and other miscellaneous items, and $15,000,000 which are to be charged to the financial management; for interest on shares, paid annually to shareholders; charges and interest accruing on loans.

In August, 1869, the company estimated that $6,000,000 more would be required to secure a uniform depth for the canal. In a word, that the work might be completely accomplished. It is to be observed here that all the materials required were to be found on the spot, and that not only was the engineer corps ready organized for use, but the necessary labor was at hand. The latter part of the work was, in consequence, less costly, in proportion, than the first. In case it should become desirable to increase the adopted proportions of the canal, this additional work, for these reasons, would cost a relatively small part of the sum expended for the whole construction. This is the opinion expressed on this point by the contractors of the canal, Messrs. Lavalley & Co., in a letter addressed to the Society of Civil Engineers, at Paris, published in 1869.

In admitting that the sum of $6,000,000 should be necessary to finish the canal and put it in perfect working order, we find that the cost of the whole work, complete, would be but $70,000,000.

Cr.	*Francs.*
Capital (500 fr. on the 400,000 shares subscribed)	200,000,000.00
Indemnity fixed by arbitration of the Emperor	84,000,000.00
Loan of 100,000,000 (300 fr. on the 333,333 bonds subscribed)	99,999,900.00
Value of grants settled by the convention of 23d August, 1869, between the Egyptian government and the company, 30,000,000; from which, deducting value of property previously purchased, there remains	29,744,530.80
Received from various sources	
Receipts anterior to formation of the company	6.504.88
Products of temporary investments, 1859-1868	18,440,938.64
Products of temporary investments, 1869	502,637.46
From various sources	559,397.85
Accessory proceeds	7,617,745.50
Receipts connected with the works	401.70
Receipts—Transportation department, 1866-'69	3,421,390.95
Receipts—Sanitary department, 1868	84,371.21
Receipts—Postal and Telegraph department, 1868-'69	65,635.37
Receipts from domain	573,625.72
Current account of domain	168.270.94
Creditors (various)	6,471,310.08
Total	$451,656,661.10

When we consider the difficulties inherent in the region in which the work has been effected, the great mechanical agencies which have been employed, the augmentation of expenses by reason of the distance of the isthmus from the base of supplies, fuel, hydraulic lime and other materials; when we take into account the obstacles of a different nature, and the delays caused thereby, which have prolonged the work beyond the time originally estimated, we are astonished at the smallness of the expense, and we are compelled to do justice to the genius and science of the men who have devoted their energies to this work, and we are forced to do homage to the excellent management which has accomplished so many and such diverse achievements with a capital so comparatively small. This is an example which is to be commended to the imitation of the leading men of our great enterprises on this side of the Atlantic.

COMMERCIAL ADVANTAGES TO BE DERIVED FROM THE SUEZ CANAL.

It would be difficult to indicate here, with any accuracy, all the modifications which will be effected by the Suez canal in the commercial relations of the East and West, and in the economy of industry and commerce, in general, in Europe. Of the two great isthmuses of the world, the penetration of which nature has delegated to our own generation, that of Suez possesses the greatest apparent importance by reason of its geographical situation. The removal of the barrier, which has been broken after a labor of ten years, opens to the whole of Europe a shorter route to Asia, lessening the distances to the Asiatic ports from 6,000 to 10,000 miles. The commerce of Europe with the countries, the access to which is thus facilitated, is larger than that which it possesses with those regions with which it would acquire an easier communication by means of a water way through that central portion of America which constitutes the other great isthmus of the world. This same European commerce is also more important than is that which America herself possesses with those countries which an American ship canal would bring nearer to her ports. It was thus natural that the first isthmus to be pierced should be that of Suez.

In 1860 the maritime movement between Europe and the East by way of the cape amounted to 7,250,000 tons. The ascertained rate of progress would give for 1870 a total of 11,000,000 tons. Taking these facts into consideration it is calculated that 6,000,000 tons may be directed through the Suez canal.

*Table showing the distances by way of the capes from prominent ports of the world to Bombay, a central point in the Indian Ocean.**

(*Distance in marine leagues, each $3\frac{45}{100}$ miles.*)

	By the Capes.	By Suez Canal.	In Favor of the Suez Canal.
PORTS.	LEAGUES.	LEAGUES.	LEAGUES.
St. Petersburg,	6,550	3,700	2,850
Amsterdam ...	5,950	3,100	2,850
Liverpool	5,900	3,050	2,850
London	5,950	3,100	2,850
Cadiz.........	5,200	2,224	2,976
Lisbon........	5,350	2,600	2,850
Havre	5,800	2,824	2,976
Marseilles.....	5,650	2,374	3,276
Trieste	5,960	2,340	3,620
Constantinople,	6,100	1,800	4,300
New York.....	6,200	3,761	2,439
New Orleans..	6,450	3,724	2,726

The change in mercantile relations will make itself evident, little by little, as is always the case in great commercial revolutions, but the gain attained by an economy of six to ten thousand miles in the distances to be traversed by shipping, is an object too considerable, at the present day, for the world not to take prompt advantage of the great innovation.

* Table contained in the *Exposé* published by M. Ferd. de Lesseps, in 1854.

We give below the "Regulations for the navigation of the Suez canal," published on the 17th August, 1869.*

The ordinary average voyages of sailing vessels between Europe and Asia, by way of the capes, are from 110 to 120 days for the outward passage, and 120 to 130 days for the return. The whole voyage, going and coming, requires an average of eight months. When we add to each trip one month in port for lading and unlading, or waiting for car-

---

* REGULATIONS FOR THE NAVIGATION OF THE SUEZ CANAL.

The following are the regulations for the navigation of this canal:

1. Navigation on the Suez maritime canal is permitted to all vessels, whatever their nationality, provided they do not draw more than seven meters and a half of water; the canal being eight meters deep. Steam vessels may navigate by means of their own steam-power; sailing vessels, above 50 tons burden, must be towed by the service established for that purpose by the company. Steamers requiring to be towed will arrange by special contract. Every vessel towed will provide its own tow-line.

2. The maximum speed of vessels on the canal is provisionally fixed at 10 kilometers per hour.

3. Every ship exceeding 100 tons burden must take a pilot employed by the company, who is bound to furnish every information as to the route to be followed, the captain remaining responsible for the conduct and handling of the vessel.

4. When a vessel requiring to pass the canal has taken up her moorings at Port Said, or at Suez, the captain is to enter his vessel at the office, and pay the passage dues, as well as the pilotage fees, towing and harbor fees, when due. A receipt will be given him which will be available in case of need. He will be bound to furnish the following particulars: Name and nationality of the vessel; name of the captain; names of the owners and charterers; port whence sailed, and destination; draft of water; number of passengers; tonnage of the ship according to the legal measurement, certified by official documents.

5. In the formation of trains, the captain, furnished with a number, according to his receipt, serving as a way-bill, and after having received the pilot on board, will take up the position assigned to him.

6. Every vessel about to enter the canal is to have her yards braced up and booms topped. She must have two anchors, one forward and one aft, to allow of anchoring at the first order of the pilot.

7. (1) Every vessel must have, during the passage of the canal, a boat in tow with a hawser ready, in order, in case of need, to carry out this hawser to one of the mooring piles placed along the two banks of the canal. (2) The captain is bound to keep watches on deck both night and day, to be ready to cast off or cut the tow-line at the first order. (3) During the night vessels will keep lights burning, according to regulation, and a look-out forward. (4) Every steam-tug or other steamer, will whistle at the passage of curves, at the approach of vessels which are to be passed or crossed, and at the approach of dredging or other engines which they may meet. (5) When two vessels, proceeding in opposite directions, come in sight, they are to slacken speed, each keeping the starboard bank, or stop, according to the order of the pilot. (6) When a vessel requires to pass another going in the same direction, warning must be given by signal. The vessel going at least speed is to keep close to the starboard bank, and to slacken speed as much as possible.

8. Vessels, which for any cause whatever are obliged to stop in the canal, are, as soon

go, the duration of a complete voyage becomes not less than ten months.

We find by the tables of commerce and navigation, that the average cargo in the trade between Europe and Asia is about five hundred tons per vessel, and that the average value per ton is $200. With the diminution of the average duration of the voyages one half, by means of the Suez canal, allowing still a month in port at either terminus, the time consumed is reduced to six months instead of ten. The expenses of transportation, varying with the duration of the voyages, will be reduced in like proportion. To make this point still clearer, we give below two tables prepared by M. A. de Chaucel, one of the promoters of the

---

as possible, to place themselves on the windward bank, and moor fore and aft. (2) In case of necessary stoppage, and when it is impossible to reach a siding, which is always to be done if possible, the captain must immediately give notice by signals by day and by lamps at night, fore and aft. (3) In case of grounding, the agents of the company will have the right to direct the means of getting the vessel off, and, if necessary, of unloading the whole at the expense of whoever may have caused the grounding.

9. Captains are forbidden (1) to anchor in the canal, except in cases of absolute necessity, and without the pilot's consent. (2) To throw into the canal earth, ashes, cinders, or any other materials. (3) In case of anything falling into the canal, a declaration is to be made to the pilot, who is bound to transmit it to the agent at the nearest station. (4) The captain is forbidden to fish up anything fallen into the canal, except under the direction of the company's agents. (5) The salvage of all objects fallen into the canal is at the expense of the captain, to whom they will be restored on payment of those expenses.

10. Captains will bind themselves, on receiving a copy of these regulations, to obey every order for the purpose of carrying them out.

11. The dues to be paid are calculated on the actual tonnage of the vessel, both as to transit dues and the towing and harbor dues. This tonnage is determined (until further orders) by the official papers on board. The transit due from one sea to the other is 10 f. per ton burden, and 10 f. per passenger, payable at the entrance at Port Said or Suez; the towage dues are fixed at 2 f. per ton; the harbor dues for anchoring at Port Said, at Ismaila, and before the platform at Suez, after remaining 24 hours, or 20 days at the utmost, five centimes per ton per day, at the place assigned by the captain of the port.

The pilotage dues for the passage of the canal are fixed according to the draft of water, as follows: Up to three meters, 5 francs per decimeter; from 3 to 4½ meters, 10 francs; from 4½ to 6 meters, 15 francs; from 6 to 7½ meters, 20 francs. Every decimiter to be paid for proportionally according to the category to which the vessel belongs.

The pilot, kept on board, in case of anchorage, will be paid 20 francs per day. Vessels towed will be entitled to a reduction of 25 per cent. on the pilotage dues.

FERD. de LESSEPS, President Directeur.

Paris, 17th August, 1869.

canal, and which were published by M. Lesseps, at the time when the Suez canal project was under discussion.*

* VOYAGE BY WAY OF THE CAPE.—Cost of a voyage, going and coming, requiring for ten months time the equipment of a ship of 500 tons.

1st.—Interest on capital represented by the value of the ship, supposing the same to be new and fully equipped. A ship of 500 tons cost, in such condition, on an average, 250,000 francs, say at 5 per cent. per annum, 12,500 francs, and for ten months, ... fr. 10,411

2nd.—Insurance. Marine insurances are made either for a given voyage, in which case the premium varies with the special risks supposed to attend the trip in question; or they are made by the year, in which case no limit is assigned to the course to be taken by the ship. The latter method is preferred for India voyages, the return of which is affected by the uncertainty of obtaining freight. The rate of insurance at 5 per cent. on the valuation, say for ten months, ... fr. 10,411

3rd.—Depreciation of hull and rigging, and redemption of capital invested. This element of expense is 10 per cent. in America; in England and France, 7 per cent. say, per annum, 18.750 fr., and for ten months,.... fr. 15,625

4th.—Wages of the crew for a voyage of ten months, varying from 9,000 fr. in England to 15,000 in France, say on an average,........ fr. 12,000

5th.—Cost of provisions varies from 12,000 fr. in France, to 24,000 fr. in England, say, on an average,........ fr. 18,000

6th.—Insurance on freight, varies very decidedly for the outward and homeward voyages, according to the nature of the merchandise, but taking a mean valuation of 1,000 fr. per ton, we may assume the outward rate at from ½ per cent. to 3 per cent. average 2 per cent. upon 500,000 fr..... fr. 10,000

On the return trip, the rate is from 3 to 6 per cent. on an average, 4½ per cent., on 500,000 fr........ fr. 22,500

7th.—Interest on capital represented by the merchandise is calculated at 5 per cent. The voyage to and from the Indies requires two periods of five months each, or one of ten, on a capital of 500,000 fr., say for ten months,........ fr. 20,833

Total, Fr. 119,780

Say Fr. 120,000 for the transportation of 1,000 tons, or Fr. 120 per ton.

VOYAGE BY WAY OF SUEZ.—Cost of a voyage, going and coming, requiring for six months the equipment of a vessel of 500 tons.

1st.—Interest on capital represented by the value of the ship, as above, 6 months,........	fr. 6,250
2d.—Insurance 6 months,........	fr. 6,250
3d.—Depreciation, etc., 6 months,........	fr. 9,375
4th.—Wages, etc., 6 months,........	fr. 7,200
5th.—Provisions, 6 months,........	fr. 10,800
6th.—Insurance on freight, 6 months,........	fr. 19,500
7th.—Interest on capital represented by cargo, 6 months,........	fr, 12,493
Total, Fr.	71,868

Say Fr. 72,000 for the transportation of 1,000 tons, or Fr. 72 per ton,........

Cost per ton by way of the cape,........	fr. 120
By way of Suez,........	fr. 72
Difference in favor of Suez,........	fr. 48

Or, in round numbers, Fr. 50 per ton.

Extract from "*Documents Statistiques Maritimes et Commericaux*" published by M. Ferd. de Lesseps, in 1856.

It appears from the figures of these tables that the cost per ton for a ship and cargo by way of the cape, with a voyage of ten months, is $24, whilst the same voyage by way of the Suez canal, with a voyage of six months, costs but $14 per ton. The saving effected by the canal for a voyage, going and returning, is thus represented by $10 per ton.

The objection which may be raised, at present against the varying uniformity in the depth of the canal, if such variation exists, is one which may safely be regarded as of but temporary application as concerns even the passage of vessels requiring the maximum depth. The well understood interests of the company are themselves a sure guaranty that all such difficulties will be satisfactorily removed. On the other hand, M. Lavalley, the contractor of the canal, declares that there need be no apprehension on this score, as the cost of obtaining the object in view will be small in proportion to the advantage to be gained.

The navigation of the Red sea has frequently been represented as opposing obstacles of a serious nature, and the question has been widely discussed of late. The truth is, that at present very little is known of the navigation of the Red sea, and, as has been well said by M. Barthelemy St. Hilaire in his publication in 1856, the old Latin maxim well applies, "*Omme ignotum pro magnifico habent.*" If, however, we were to judge by the remarkable regularity of the English mail service, since the establishment of its connection with Suez, we would have little to fear. The difficulties, if they exist, may be more especially applicable to sailing vessels. The question of the availability and safety of the Red sea has been thoroughly elucidated by the investigations of Captain Harris, of the British merchant service, who has made seventy voyages between Calcutta and Suez. He was nominated, on behalf of England, as a member of the international Commission, in 1855, and declares that, from Ras Mohammed to the Straits of Bab el Mendeb, the Red sea offers no greater difficulties in the way of navigation than does the Mediterranean. This opinion was quoted in the report presented to the Viceroy of Egypt, in 1862, by G. Hawkshaw, Vice-President of the Institution of Civil Engineers, in London, in which he gives the weight of his high reputation to other objections which have been brought forward: such as that the canal would become a mere stagnant ditch; that it would be filled up with mud and with the moving sands of the desert; that the Bitter lakes, through which the canal passes, would be filled up with salt; that the ships would fear to approach Port Said because of the difficulty of that approach and the dangers of the lee shore there; and finally, that it would be difficult, if not impossible, to keep the passage from the Mediterranean into the canal open. Concerning the latter two arguments, experience has already come to the assistance of prophetic science. Port Said has become, even before the opening of the ship canal, the rendezvous of numerous fleets, and it may be borne in mind that, since 1856, an interoceanic communication has been maintained, by way of the canal from Port Said to Ismaila, and from there by means of the sweet water canal to Suez.

It may be admitted that the navigation of the Red sea cannot be compared with that of the ocean, as to the facilities which sailing vessels there obtain for their required movements. Periods of calm and of persistent contrary winds will assuredly interfere with navigation, but this does not constitute an insuperable obstacle, as the employment of steam-tugs will sufficiently provide for all emergencies. This means will, indeed, require a certain expenditure, but, thanks to the opening of the ship canal, fuel is cheap on the Red sea, and the steam-tug service can be cheaplyrendered by reason of the large number of the vessels which will require it. The question of calms and contrary winds on the Red sea, considered by itself with reference to sailing vessels, has, therefore, not at all the importance which one would be inclined to accord to it at first sight.

In order to comprehend fully this subject, we must take into account the process of transformation which is steadily going forward in the merchant marine, in the substitution for larger vessels of those of smaller draft and more manageable proportions. The Suez canal will, undoubtedly, do much to hasten this change. The large vessels now employed in the commerce of the East will, in due time, be replaced by others of smaller dimensions, better adapted to a transit which resembles that of an inland sea. The great distance to be traversed and the condition of the trade in former days naturally led to the construction of immense hulks, but to-day, when the channel of communication is easier and shorter, even for their bulky cargoes, and the market is more sensitive and fluctuating, merchants will prefer shipments of reduced size and greater frequency. The heavy consignments were possible only under a monopoly. At the present time the East is not only readily accessible, but is open to all, and commerce is more generally diffused. Individual ventures will be less in amount, but their number will be multiplied. This is one important result of the improvement in the routes of transit.

While ships of excessive tonnage are laid aside, there is a growing tendency to substitute steam for sails, or to employ vessels which combine the two. The increase already effected in the number of steamers over sailing vessels is certainly beyond all expectation. At Alexandria, in 1866, the number of steamers was 1,350 to 800 sailing vessels; in 1868 it was 1,500 to 700. The number of sailing vessels built in England in the year 1867, as compared with those of 1865, showed a decrease of 71 ships, with a decrease in the total tonnage of that class of ships of 33,124 tons, while the increase of steamers was 113, with an increased tonnage of 52,152 tons. The impulse given to commerce by the application of steam to navigation and overland transportation, tends daily to a greater extension of its requirements and to render necessary a greater promptness and certainty of delivery than can be secured by sailing vessels.

In the remarkable report of the Commissioners of the Government of Holland, upon the results of the opening of the Suez canal, published in 1860, it is said, with good reason, "It is certain that, after the penetration of the isthmus of Suez by this channel, the commerce of the ports of the Mediterranean with the East Indies *will be transacted exclusively in steam vessels.*" If this prediction shall be realized, the ocean ports will follow this movement. When the oriental cargoes shall begin to arrive at Marseilles, by the Suez route, not only by means of steam alone, but by combined sail and steam, from Ceylon in 37 days, from Singapore in 49 days; from Java in 50 days; and when cargoes from Marseilles shall reach Ceylon in 34 days, Singapore in 43, and Java in 45, it will no longer be possible for the ocean merchants to allow their ships to sail slowly over the sea by way of the cape, in order to reach the Lizzard from Ceylon and Singapore in 116 days, and from Java in 110.

We must, on the other hand, confess that the application of steam to the navigation of the Suez route is greatly facilitated by the ease with which coal can be supplied at the successive stations. Vessels can coal at the Mediterranean ports, and again at Suez, and still further at Aden, sufficing for the whole voyage to Bombay or Calcutta. Owing to this circumstance, a much larger proportionate space on shipboard can be devoted to the transportation of paying freight, and that is an advantage not to be despised.

Independent of the regular transit through the canal, twenty-six steamers, forming several regular lines, arrive monthly at Port Said, and on the Red sea, regular steam lines exist from Suez to the East, comprising twelve departures and arrivals. These numbers are comparatively small, but remarkable as the instantaneous fruit of the opening of the canal.

M. Lesseps, in his report to the stockholders of the canal, in 1869, expressed himself in the following manner, concerning the future resources of the enterprise, after having enumerated the several great transportation companies in Europe, which were preparing to avail themselves of the new route:

"The commercial statistics of the Chinese ports, give us an idea of what the canal may expect from the existing relations between the Occident and the Orient. The total value of the imports and exports of the Chinese Empire, which was, in 1855, 281,000,000 fr., amounted, in 1868, to 1,120,000,000. The number of vessels entering and clearing, in 1855, was 1,527, with a measurement of 529,222 tons, and, in 1868, 14,075, with a measurement of 6,418,503 tons.

"We said, last year, that Marseilles had an annual tonnage of 5,000,000, Liverpool of 6.000,000, and the Dardanelles, leading into a closed sea, of 6,000,000 tons.

"From these figures we see that the amount of 6,000,000 tons, claimed in our preceding report, would be but a feeble minimum for the shipping of all the maritime world which would use the canal. We retain it, however, because the certainty of a gross receipt of 60,000,000 fr. greatly surpasses the revenue anticipated at the inception of our enterprise."

The United States, till we possess our own canal, will share largely in the transformation which the Suez canal will effect in the commerce of the world.

Our trade with the following countries for the fiscal year ending June, 1867, was as follows:

	Exports.	Imports.
Dutch East Indies............	$204,395	
British East Indies............	381,141	$3,932,485
Australia....................	5,102,355	262,401
Phillippine Islands............	45,636	3,473,371
Other Pacific Islands..........	85,137	
China........................	8,788,145	12,112,440
Total	$14,606,809	$19,780,697

As Cadiz would be one of the ports of call for any steamship line from this country to Suez, it may be added that it is at the same distance from New York as Liverpool, and that the voyage can be made in less time, on account of the favorable weather prevailing on that route. The voyage from New York to Suez, including detentions at the usual places of call, can be made in sixteen days. The opening of the canal must evidently be favorable to American commerce. A part of such eastern products as are consumed in this country have reached us, up to the present time, by way of Liverpool, and we may now hope for a more direct communication with the East.

We publish underneath a tabular schedule embracing the main points of the charges which will be incurred by vessels navigating the Suez canal, as set forth in the eleventh clause of the tariff rules exhibit issued by M. Ferdinand de Lesseps, in Paris, on the 17th of August, and published *in extenso* in the *New York Herald* of the 18th of September, 1869.*

THE AMERICAN ISTHMUS CONSIDERED WITH REFERENCE TO A SHIP CANAL.

The isthmus of Suez is an arid, sandy, longitudinal depression of but a hundred miles in width. More than one half of it is on a level with, or below, the Red sea and the Mediterranean. The surface presents but a succession of swamps and lagoons, and an expanse of drifting sand, with scarcely an elevation whose main height is more than

---

* TABLE OF DUES PAYABLE BY VESSELS TRAVERSING THE SUEZ CANAL.

Transit dues, per ton burden, 10 f. or $2.

Transit dues, per passenger, 10 f. or $2.

Towage dues, per ton, 2 f. or 40 cents.

Vessels anchoring at Port Said, Ismaila, or before the platform at Suez, after the first twenty-four hours, are to pay a tax of 5 centimes, or 1 cent, per ton per day, for any period not exceeding twenty-days.

	Francs.	Dollars.
Pilotage dues for 3 meters (9 ft. 10 in.), per decimeter or 3 93-100 inches	5	or 1
Pilotage dues for 3 to 4½ meters (9 ft. 10 in. to 14 ft. 9 in.), per decimeter, or 3 93-100 inches	10	" 2
Pilotage dues for 4½ to 6 meters (14 ft. 9 in. to 19 ft. 8 in.) per decimeter, or 3 93-100 inches	15	" 3
Pilotage dues for 6 and 7½ meters (19 ft. 8 in. to 24 ft. 7 in.), per decimeter, or 3 93-100 inches	20	" 4

All fractions to be paid for in proportion.

A vessel of 1,000 tons burden, carrying 100 passengers and drawing say twenty-four feet seven inches, or seven and a half meters, will consequently have to pay as follows:

Tonnage dues at $2 per ton, on 1,000 tons	$2,000
100 passengers at $2 per head	200
Draught of water, 7½ meters, or 24 ft. 7 in., at $4 per decimeter (3 93-100 inches)	300
Total transit charges	$2,500

The charge for pilots, if detained on board during the anchorage, per day Fr. 20 or $4

Vessels being towed are entitled to a reduction of twenty-five per cent. on the pilotage dues.

fifty feet. The American isthmus, on the contrary, is traversed, for its whole length, by the chain of the Cordilleras, with occasional peaks of from two to nine thousand feet in height, and whose least depression gives an altitude of from two hundred to six hundred feet. The one isthmus is a sandy desert, the other a volcanic ridge having in some places but a small area of alluvial formation. The contrast is striking, not only in the aspect of the country, but in the formation of the soil itself.

We see thus, at the first glance, that the American isthmus generally lacks the natural advantages which have facilitated the penetration of the isthmus situated in the other hemisphere. The localities, where the explorations and surveys described in the first Chapter have been prosecuted, vary in width from fifty to one hundred and fifty miles. Those, where the two seas most nearly approach one another, are formed almost exclusively by the chain of the Cordilleras, which constitutes the backbone of the isthmus, as at Darien and Panama. In those parts, where the isthmus becomes wider, the slopes of the mountain ranges are prolonged by alluvial formations, as in all that part situated north of Costa Rica. Will it be the wider or the narrower part of the Isthmus whose adaptability will lead to its selection as the locality of the proposed canal? The question is complex. There is, on one hand, the configuration and geography of the country, which will decide the system to be employed in the construction of the canal, and, on the other hand, there are reasons of commerce, of state and of political economy, which must influence the selection of the precise locality,

The Government of the United States has recently undertaken to aid in the elucidation of these questions. With this view an expedition has sailed, some months since, to make a new reconnoissance upon the isthmus of Darien. The solution of the problem by the construction of a "thorough cut" seems to have especially occupied the attention of the government, and it is in order to have the latest information as to the feasibility of such an undertaking, under conditions relatively reasonable, that the present examination of Darien is being made. It is natural that, with reference to the construction of a "thorough cut," our attention should be first directed to the narrowest part of the Isthmus, but we must also consider that this is precisely the point which is most distant from our own frontiers, and the least adapted to serve the relations between the opposite coasts of the Uuited States. If, on the contrary, a canal with locks is in question, the latter point could certainly be dealt with in a more satisfactory manner by a more northerly location. We do not believe that there exists at Darien a summit level supplied with sufficient water for a canal with locks. At Panama the surveys of M. Garella have informed us that an adequate supply cannot be obtained there. We are therefore compelled to come higher up, at least as for as Nicaragua, or better still, to Tehuantepec, to find a solution of our problem; and there every required advantage could be secured for our national and commercial interests.

The "thorough cut" would be certainly the better and more commodious means of effecting the junction of the two seas, but, independently of the circumstance that it would necessarily be made in a latitude, which would occasion for our home navigation a considerable detour, we must also take into account the large expenditure which such an undertaking would require. In the first Chapter, which contains a description of the several canal projects now before the public, we have given the estimates made for the proposed "thorough cuts." The first is that of M. Trautwine, referring to a line by way of the Atrato and San Juan rivers, amounting to $325,000,000; the second, that of Mr. James C. Lane, relative to another line connecting with the Atrato river, presents an estimated cost of $150,000,000; after that we have the calculation for the "thorough cut" at Darien, from Caledonia bay to the gulf of San Miguel, suggested by Dr. Cullen; this estimate, made in Paris upon pure hypothesis, amounts to Fr. 135,000,000, and may not be considered worthy of serious discussion. We have also to mention the estimate of M. L. de Puydt for a canal of fifty-five miles, in the same region, from Port Escondido, in the direction of the Tuyra river, to the gulf of San Miguel. The amount called for by this estimate is $70,000,000 ; but we are compelled to add that, as no complete survey of this route is in existence, a great many things are necessarily left to be decided by circumstances. On an examination of all the information which we possess at the present day, we are satisfied that immense expense will certainly be involved in the execution of a "thorough cut" at any point. Other data will undoubtedly be presented as a result of the expedition now in operation, but what is already known of the geology and topography of Darien leaves us no hope of a more favorable reply.

Meantime, the example of the Suez canal affords us a point of comparison which may be employed with a good deal of fairness, in order to form a correct opinion of the magnitude of the work and expense of which an American interoceanic canal without locks would be sure to require. The cost of construction of the Suez canal, with its hundred miles of excavation and the works at its two ports, amounts to $70,000,000, as we have seen in the first part of this Chapter. A quantity of excavation and dredging of 75,000,000 cubic meters had been accomplished at the time of opening the canal, and about 5,000,000 more were required to give to the canal a uniform depth of twenty-six feet. We have, thus, over 80,000,000 cubic meters or 105,000,000 cubic yards for the whole work. Suppose an American canal of fifty miles in length, we have the cut effected at Suez reduced one-half. Deducting further, one-third, on account of the greater compactness of the soil, requiring a less slope at the margins, we find 35,000,000 cubic yards of excavation necessary for the bed of the American canal and its ports. Concerning these latter, however much nature may have done for them, they will, nevertheless, require artificial improvements, the cost of which will counterbalance such excavation as may not be called for. Let us now take notice that no serious obstacle upon the surface of the isthmus at Suez stood in the way of the operations, and that two-thirds of the canal was dredged through lagoons and swamps, whilst upon the American isthmus we shall be compelled to pierce the Cordilleras. Suppose that a passage should be discovered where the depression is greater than at any point which is known at this day, the excavation required above the level of the sea would not be less, probably, than the cubic matter which would be removed to form the bed of the canal. There will thus be a total removal, above and below the level of the sea, of 70,000,000 cubic yards, to be effected in a rocky soil, where the porphyritic formation will probably be encountered. What will be the sum which such an excavation as this will cost, including materials and all the other expenses attending the enterprise? One may fix it at least at $85,000,000. We will explain this figure by the following calculation.

There are included in the sum of $70,000,000, expended for the construction of the Suez canal, as we have seen by the detailed accounts given: first, the sum of $1,000,000 for the expenses of the organization of the enterprise, and $7,000,000 more, absorbed in materials for construction and different establishments. There remain, in consequence, $62,000,000, which constitute, properly speaking, the cost of construction, with an excavation of 105,000,000 cubic yards. Supposing, now, a similar sum of $8,000,000, to be required for like purposes in connection with the American canal—and there are no reasons why this should not be so—there will remain from the $85,000,000 above indicated, $77,000,000 for the execution of the work of the American canal. This figure is only a very moderate one when it is intended to excavate 70,000,000 cubic yards, a large part of which will require mining and blasting, and we doubt that the work ever could be done for such a sum.

The Suez Canal Company has paid, during the time consumed in the construction of their work, $15,000,000 interest on the capital engaged in the enterprise. This interest was generally calculated at five per cent. For the American canal we must allow at least 7 per cent., the rate of the loans of the large industrial enterprises of this country. The American enterprise will certainly not meet with the obstacles which have so greatly prolonged the construction of the Suez canal, but, on the other hand, the greater difficulties to be overcome, and the accumulation of the work upon a lesser extent of surface, may prolong the operations in such a manner that, taking into account the greater rate of interest, the sum paid for interest during the construction of the American canal will probably not be less than that disbursed by the Suez company. Adding, therefore, the sum of $15,000,000 for this purpose to that, which we have indicated as the cost of construction, we have a grand total of $100,000,000, as the sum required for the construction of a thorough cut American canal under the conditions which we have described.

This estimate, superficial as it may be, is otherwise confirmed by a calculation based upon other premises.

Admitting, which is hardly possible, that the American line should measure only thirty miles, and adopting for the canal a depth of 26 feet and a width at the surface of 300, and of 222 at the bottom, we find that, to form the bed of the canal, an excavation of 1,364,444 cubic yards per mile will be required. This quantity, multiplied by thirty, makes 40,933,320 cubic yards.

We will assume that the removal above the level of the canal will but equal that below it, and we obtain a total quantity of 81,866,640 cubic yards for the "thorough cut" of 30 miles, without its ports. The figure of $85,000,000 made up of 8,000,000 for materials and expenses of organization, and $77,000,000 for the work, properly so called, is thus again justified. Adding $15,000,000 which would be paid for interest upon the capital involved in the great enterprise, we have a total, again, of $100,000,000, to be made productive by the operation of the canal.

If we are well informed, the earnings of the Suez Canal, from November 17th to January 31st, last. may have been £23,000. This, a little more than $46,000 per month, would make for twelve months $552,000. It would be unjust to estimate the future revenue of this great enterprise by the results of the first few months of its actual operation.* We should rather adopt a figure ten times as large to value the receipts of the first years after its opening, and which certainly will, in four or five years, increase at least fifty per cent. more, and after that in proportion to the general growth and development of commerce. We would thus have for the first years $5,520,000, and, after four or five years, something like $8,000,000. This would suppose, at first, a tonnage of 2,760,000, and, in four or five years, a tonnage of 4,000,000. Deducting the expenses of working and general administration, there would remain a yearly net revenue, after a period of four or five years, of seven to eight per cent. for the capital invested, independently of auxiliary resources special to the Suez enterprise.

The same movement for an American canal, costing $100,000,000, would produce a revenue of six to seven per

---

Statement of Ships passed through the Suez Canal from November 20, 1869, to April 30, 1870, (161 days):

English Ships	94
French "	19
Egyptian "	16
Austrian "	6
Italian "	2
Russian "	2
Spanish "	2
Turkish "	2
Total number of ships	143

(*Courrier du Commerce, du 22 Mai,* 1870,)

From a list published in the " *Le Canal de Suez*," a weekly paper of Paris, we see that besides the ships of the regular established lines, the clearances in April and May 1870, from the principal ports of Asia and Europe, for the Suez Canal, show 37 steamers of a total register of 433,519 tons, with the following destination:

From East India to England	11	steamers.
" " France	2	"
" " Italy	1	"
To " from England	12	"
" " France	1	"
" " Italy	1	"
From China and Japan to England	6	"
" " France	3	"
Total	37	"

(*Le Canal de Suez, May 26th,* 1870.)

cent., supposing the earnings would be the same; but it is at this time easy to see that the traffic of the American canal will not before a long time amount to half of that of the Suez, therefore, a capital of $100,000,000, or even of $75,000,000, invested in an American canal, would for a long time obtain no more than two or three per cent. per annum.

CHAPTER THIRD.

The problem to be solved by an American Ship Canal.

It is sufficient to cast a glance at that part of the chart of the world in which our hemisphere appears, to be struck with the peculiar shape of the American continent. It is the longest continent in the world. It extends from 70° north of the equator to 50° south, while Africa, the other part of the world which projects furthest south from the equator, attains only 35°. No natural means of water communication from coast to coast exists in the interior, and the extraordinary development to the southward offers an exceptional impediment to circumnavigation. To the North and to the South there are two vast expanses of *terra firma*, of which the greatest transverse width is more than three thousand miles. In the centre, where are the gulf of Mexico and the Caribbean sea, there is an isthmus more than fifteen hundred miles in length, which invites the ingenuity of man to establish an artificial communication across the narrow neck of land, in order to avoid the long voyage around the cape from one coast to the other. We have demonstrated in the preceding Chapter, how much the geographical situation of the isthmus of Suez favored the establishment of a channel of communication between Europe and Asia. It is not to meet the requirements of Asiatico-European commerce, that a transit through the American isthmus is to-day demanded, but on the contrary, it is mainly for American commerce in America, and its commercial connections with the Orient, that such a canal is desirable if not indispensable.

Our national territory, which at first was bounded on the West by the Rocky mountains, has in these latter days extended to the shores of the Pacific, and is now bounded on the South by the gulf of California (*mar de Cortez*), and the Rio Grande. Communication between our ports on the Atlantic and those of the Pacific requires protracted voyages. The distance from New York to San Francisco, for example, is over fourteen thousand miles, by sea. The moment we are able to penetrate the Isthmus, we have cleft America in twain, and we can pass from the north shores on the Atlantic, to the corresponding coasts of the Pacific, without needing to descend to the fiftieth degree of south latitude. This will be the first great advantage, and the most important to the United States, which will be realized by the establishment of a water transit between the coasts, more available than any railway. There is here a great question, commercial, political, social and economical, which is too clearly apparent to require elucidation; its statement alone sufficiently sets forth its importance.

The saving of time and money by the employment of a ship canal traversing our continent, with reference to the trade between our eastern and western shores, is beyond all calcu lation, by reason of the geographical position of the Atlantic and Pacific states. The distance of 14,200 miles from New York to San Francisco by way of the Cape, for example, will be reduced to 4,400 by a canal, which, for the moment, we will suppose to be located at Tehuantepec. The voyage will therefore be reduced by 9,800 miles, and the duration of the trip in a sailing vessel, which is admitted to be 150 days by way of the cape, will be not more than 45 days; difference 105 days. According to the comparative tables of cost of a voyage to San Francisco, which we give below,* the reduction in the duration of the voyage will secure an economy of $9,261 for a vessel with a crew of thirty men, and another saving of $4,042 in insurance and in interest on the capital,

---

*The saving that would be effected by the adoption of an interoceanic canal upon the isthmus may be illustrated by the following comparison of the expenditure of time and

presumed to be represented by the cargo. Finally, the total saving for a single trip would be $13,300, which, with reference to the tonnage, supposing the ship to be of 1000 tons burden, would make a saving of $13 per ton, or $26 per ton for the round trip, going and returning. Such an improvement in the conditions affecting our commercial relations with California, when the interoceanic canal is opened, would cause a revolution in the supply of food and other domestic products to our great centres of population on the Atlantic coast.

On the other hand, from San Francisco to Liverpool, the ship laden with our produce is compelled to make a voyage of 13,600 miles. The passage across the isthmus would reduce this distance to 6,600. What a feature in the agricultural development of our Pacific states will the shortened voyage to Europe offer, when we consider that, at this very moment, separated as are the producer and consumer by the distance necessitated by doubling Cape Horn, our products can nevertheless compete with similar productions in the Eu-

---

money in the passage of a ship with a crew of thirty men, from New York to California, via Cape Horn, with what it would be by way of the canal:

Time: 150 days.		Time: 45 days.	
Salaries and finding of officers and crew for 5 months,	$5,880	Salaries and finding of officers and crew for 1½ months,	$1,764
Insurance on $90,000, (value of the ship,) for 5 months	3,600	Insurance for 1½ months,	1,080
Wear, tear and depreciation at 10 per cent. per annum, for 5 months	3,750	Wear, tear and depreciation for 1½ months,	1,125
Total	$13,230	Total	$3,969

Difference in favor of the canal, 105 days, and $9,261.

Supposing the value of the cargo to be $100,000, the saving on it would be as follows:

Interest at 7 per cent. for 5 months,	$2,916	Interest at 7 per cent. for 1½ months	$874
Insurance at 4 per cent.	4,000	Insurance at 2 per cent.	2,000
Total	$6,916	Total	$2,874

Difference in favor of a canal, $4,042.

The total gain of ship and cargo would therefore be, $13,303.

With respect to the cargo it would avoid the damage of goods going round Cape Horn—at present a very heavy percentage on their value. (*Extract of a Memoir on the Isthmus Canal, published by "Engineering," London, Volume V, 1st Semester*, 1868.

ropean markets! From California to the eastern coast of South America, as, for example, to Rio Janeiro, we have to traverse a distance of 9,200 miles, being always under the necessity of doubling the Cape, whilst by way of the Isthmus the products of our Pacific slope, destined for Brazil, would only be conveyed 4,500 miles.

Passing from our internal commerce, and from the consideration of our agricultural exports, to the question of importation and exchange, which has, as yet, hardly made a beginning with the western coast of South America, we immediately perceive the bearing of a water transit across the Isthmus. The new route will bring our eastern ports exceptionally near to those of western South America, the commerce of which is at the present time almost all absorbed by Europe. We have actually 8,700 miles to traverse in going from our Atlantic ports to Valparaiso, and 9,900 to Callao. New York will not be further from these ports than England, when the passage through the Isthmus shall be opened, and the voyage from our commercial metropolis to these ports will be reduced nearly one half for the first, and two-thirds for the second. In fact, the western coast of South America will be brought so near to our Atlantic ports that we shall necessarily, in part at least, supplant Europe in their commerce.

Lieut. Maury in a letter written to Hon. M. Rockwell, some twenty years ago, says upon this question: "Owing of the course of winds, the direction of currents and other physical circumstances, British merchants are ten days sail and upwards nearer than we are to all the markets of the world, except those of the Caribbean sea and gulf of Mexico. They are next door to all the markets of Europe, to Brazil, to Cape Horn, to the Cape of Good Hope; and consequently, to all the ports beyond them, they are practicaly some ten or fifteen days sail nearer than we are. A vessel from the United States bound to the southern hemisphere , first sails nearly an east course until she arrives in the vicinity of the Azores and Canary islands; she then puts her head south for the first time. Now, while the

American vessel is sailing this route, the English vessel that sailed on the same day, for the same market, has passed those islands and is far on her way, for the reason that the Cape Verde islands are somė ten or fifteen days nearer to England than to America, England is that much nearer to the southern hemisphere; for vessels generally, whether from the United States or from England, are in the habit of passing by these islands in their way thither."

Thus, whichever way we turn, appears the utility—we may say at this day the necessity—of a means of communication, which shall admit of a continuous voyage, without breaking cargo, considered only from the point of view of the relations between the coasts of our continent. The passage, which will give us access to the Pacific, will lead our ships with the same facility to Australia, the Sandwich islands, Japan and China; as it will in each case avoid the detour around Cape Horn. We gain one fourth in the voyage to Melbourne, half of the actual distance of the voyage from New York to Honolulu, and more than one-third for Yokohama and Shanghai.

A branch of our national industry, that of the whaling fishery, will also, by the opening of an isthmian canal, obtain the means of changing completely the method which until now it has been compelled to employ. The actual "seasons" of three years will be shortened, although reaching the same returns. The earnings of the fishery will be every year brought to the Atlantic ports at a smaller cost, and a complete revolution is to be looked for, which will tend greatly to foster that fishery, by offering greater net profits than are now obtained, and by rendering this industry better adapted to men of small capital.

There is, in the effect to be produced upon the future commerce of the world by the opening of the two isthmuses, a marked difference between the canal of the Asiatico-African isthmus and that of the American. The former is destined to facilitate the commerce of two great divisions of the globe, the one with the other, while the American canal is at first to radiate its influence over the American continent itself, and in the second place, to serve the commerce of Australia, Japan and China with our Atlantic ports. For the same reason it will serve to bring European commerce more readily to the western shores of the new world, and will also aid, under certain circumstances, the commerce of Europe with the eastern part of Asia.

We frequently hear it said, since the subject of an American interoceanic canal has been under discussion, that the United States, placed as they are between Europe and Asia, should monopolize the trade between those two continents, by means of the proposed canal. It would be equally unreasonable to say that, because the Suez canal is situated in Africa, midway between Europe and Asia, that part of the world should monopolize the Asiatico-European commerce. Such ideas can only arise from recollections of vanished political economy. Rapid means of communication, of which the application constitutes a grand feature of our age, present this peculiarity, that they have enfranchised the commerce of the world from the oppressive transit charges with which it was burdened in other times. In proportion to the extent of the relations, they become more direct with the facilities which we possess to-day, and the greatest distances are accomplished without touching at intermediate points. None of the interoceanic canals will become a centre of commerce or of exchange; they will be places of passage, and the commerce of Europe and Asia, with reference to an American canal and to the commerce of the United States, must be considered simply as in "transit," and concerning this fact we cannot be mistaken.

We often err, nowadays, in the signification we give to the word "transit," the true meaning of which, commercially, refers to the *act of passing through* a region or country. The question of "transit" under the old system of political economy possessed a peculiar importance, and was always a matter for weighty consideration among statesmen in the days when we had not yet attained those highly perfected means of transportation which have effected a change, in more than one respect, in the ancient customs of commerce.

First, the sovereign of any country exacted and received transit duties for the transportation of merchandise across his territory. Again, the transit formed a source of revenue to the people themselves, and governments were jealous to preserve this advantage to their subjects. Government even, in some cases, undertook to regulate the mode itself, and the stages by which transit should be accomplished. The navigation of the Rhine, one of the finest rivers of Germany, for instance, was, prior to 1830, regulated in a singular manner by its riparian governments. The colonial productions shipped through Holland by way of the Rhine for the South of Germany and Switzerland, were compelled to make stoppages on the banks of the river at places designated (*Stappelplaetze*), where each cargo was broken and transferred to fresh bottoms. From Holland to Cologne, from Cologne to Mayence, from Mayence to Manheim, separate duties for navigation and transit were collected, and the goods were subjected in each of these cities to successive transferment; and this continued until the time of the declaration of the freedom of the navigation of the Rhine. France constructed the northern section of the *Canal du Rhone au Rhin* especially for the purpose of bringing through its own borders the transportation of merchandise destined for Switzerland and which ascended the Rhine to Strasbourg. In those days the question of "transit" had a genuine local importance, but at present, the question has lost its general interest when a liberal policy has done away with the fiscal duties, and when, by reason of the more perfect means of transportation, "transit" has become no longer a source of profit, whether to the local trade which it formerly created, nor to those who obtained business and employment in connection with the old highways. The commerce of the United States, for instance, would gain but very little by reason of the employment of the American canal by ships plying between Asia and Europe. This fact does not at all affect the prosperity of our commerce, it has only a certain significance, proportioned to the amount which the transit in question would contribute to the revenues of the canal. It is only from this point of view that the subject possesses any interest, but in any case, if this trade employs the American canal it would only affect the relations between Europe and eastern Asia.

The following table, furnished by the Navy Department at Washington, shows the comparative distances from Europe to Australia and eastern Asia by way of the Suez Canal and a canal across the American isthmus:

From Liverpool to	via Suez.	via American isthmus.	in favor of Suez. Naut. miles.
Hong Kong,	9,568	14,220	4,652
Shanghai,	10,368	13,820	3,452
Yokohama,	11,403	12,900	1,497
Melbourne,	11,269	12,600	1,331

We do not need to observe that the distances themselves are not to be accepted as a final argument in a discussion which involves navigation in general. However we may regard these distances as a base of argument in speaking of steam vessels, we are compelled to admit other weighty considerations when we come to deal with sailing vessels. We are well aware that the region in which the trade winds are most reliable corresponds with the American isthmus. The trade wind region extends on either side of the equator, on the Atlantic and Pacific, to the parallels of 30° north and 30° south latitude. The facility of availing of the trade winds by employing the American canal for sailing vessels between Asia and Europe may doubtless attract a part of that trade to the American isthmus; but in view of what we have said as to the change which is taking place in the construction of sailing vessels, the tendency to substitute steam for sails in long voyages, and the special facilities offered by the Suez route for steam navigation, the utility of the American canal to the Asiatico-European trade must continue still problematical. For the same reason this element in the future traffic of the canal may be only deserving a passing mention in the calculation which we have to make, in forming an estimate of the revenue upon which the capital to be invested in such an enterprise may depend.

AMERICAN SHIPPING AND TRADE INTERESTED IN THE CONSTRUCTION OF THE SHIP CANAL.

The relations between our Atlantic and Pacific states are day by day becoming of greater importance. We give below the number of ships clearing from New York for San Francisco by way of the Cape, during the last six years, as specially reported by the Custom House authorities of New York:

	Number of vessels cleared at New York.	Tonnage. Tons.
1863	77	86,486
1864	72	80,928
1865	52	57,099
1866	78	84,202
1867	85	100,021
1868	107	125,743

The trade of other of our Atlantic ports and the expeditions of goods by way of the Panama railway would probably increase these figures to over 200,000 tons.*

---

* We add the following table, in order to show the number of vessels cleared at each of our prominent ports of the Atlantic states for San Francisco, from 1856 to 1860:

From Ports.	Number of ships.	Register tons.	Tons of cargo.	Amount of freight paid.
New York,	372	456,332	730,130	$8,865,970
Boston,	179	183,628	290,508	3,519,184
Other ports	30	22,478	35,012	411,746
	581	662,438	1,055,650	$12,796,900

(Extract from "*Illustrated History of the Panama Railroad*," by E. N. Ottis.)

Average of the same clearances, per year, from 1856 to 1860:

From Ports.	Number of ships.	Register tons.	Tons of cargo.	Amount of freight paid.
New York,	74	91,266	146,026	$1,773,154
Boston,	36	36,725	58,101	703,837
Other Ports,	6	4,489	7,002	83,350
	116	132,480	211,129	$2,559,340

We have already seen that an interoceanic ship canal, located most advantageously for our own frontiers, by reducing the distance between New York and San Francisco from 14,200 to 4,400 miles, would effect a saving of 9,800 miles, shortening the voyage by more than a hundred days. This improvement would bring our manufacturers and commercial centres in the eastern states nearer to our Pacific possessions, of which the population is rapidly increasing by reason of the facility of access now supplied by the railway which, with ramifications to all our ports, stretches across the continent from the Atlantic to the Pacific. It is impossible to predict the development of commerce in this direction which would follow the construction of a ship canal, and without being accused of exaggeration, we may assume that the expeditions from the ports of the Atlantic to our sister states on the Pacific would surpass by one half our present figures after the opening of the canal.

In spite of the necessity they are under of doubling the Cape, the States of the Pacific send us the agricultural productions which their fertile soil enables them to supply in greater proportionate abundance than any other part of the Union. What will these shipments become when 45 days, instead of a 150 days, shall suffice to bring them to the shores of the Atlantic. Importations of this sort into the port of New York, have been made in

1868, by 37 vessels registered,.......... ....38,306 Tons.
1869, " 28 " " ....29,138 "

These importations are naturally subject to the fluctuations of the markets, but for all the disadvantages under which it labors at present, the agriculture of our Pacific states has been able to exert a depressing influence upon the market for cereals on the Atlantic coast. It is incontestable that whenever the cost of transportation shall have been reduced at the rate of $13,00 per ton, as compared with existing charges, the face of affairs will be sensibly changed, and our great centres of population on the eastern coast will receive in still greater quantities of the productions of the

Pacific states, and at lower prices than ever. If the producer of the West cannot prevent in our Atlantic States the importation of California cereals at the present time, for a stronger reason this importation will be continued and augmented when transportation can be effected more economically. The commerce of 200,000 tons from the Atlantic to the Pacific states will thus be compensated, if not excelled, by a corresponding tonnage furnished by the importation of the products of the Pacific. We have here, then, an internal commercial movement of 400,000 to 500,000 tons of shipping, to which the canal will afford the most important facilities.

The vessels cleared at the Pacific ports of the United States for Europe present the following statistics for the past six years:

	Number of vessels.	Tonnage. Tons.
In 1863,	28	29,416
" 1864,	34	36,362
" 1865,	22	18,250
" 1866,	22	16,883
" 1867,	129	96,472
" 1868,	148	123,632

On the other hand, the arrivals at San Francisco from Europe, for the same period were:

	Number of vessels.	Tonnage. Tons.
In 1863,	28	29,416
" 1864,	57	36,717
" 1865,	71	43,907
" 1866,	43	28,722
" 1867,	50	30,461
" 1868,	98	62,357

The distance between Europe and California by way of the Cape is 13,624 miles (from San Francisco to the Lizard), and by way of the canal would be 6,671 miles, in case the canal should be located at Tehuantepec,—difference 6,953 miles. We do not need, after what we have already said, to enlarge upon the consequences which such a reduction of distances would be sure to effect, principally in the exports of our Pacific states. The actually existing shipping between California and Europe already presents, as we see, an amount of about 200,000 tons.*

The relations of San Francisco with the Atlantic ports of South America are not at the present time of any great importance, and on examining the tables of commerce between San Francisco and that part of the world, we find only, in 1868, nine vessels, registering 2,857 tons, cleared from the Pacific ports of the United states for the Atlantic ports of South America, and seven vessels, with 5,120 tons, from these latter ports entered into San Francisco. By means of the interoceanic canal the distance from San Francisco to Rio de Janiero would be reduced by 4,500 miles. Such an economy in the voyage between the two ports would undoubtedly develop an increased volume of transactions.

Our commerce with Chili and Peru presents, according to the table of the Bureau of Statistics, of the Treasury Department, for 1869, $6,332,222.† The tonnage of this was, in 1868:

For Chili............................	49,078 tons.
" Peru............................	78,429 "
Total...............	127,507 "

We give the following table of distances from New York to the two prominent ports of the western shore of South America, by way of the Cape and by way of an interoceanic canal:

Ports.	By way of Cape Horn.	By way of an Isthmian Canal.	In favor of the interoceanic Canal. Naut. miles.
Valparaiso,......	8,720	5,000	3,720
Callao,..........	9,920	3,700	6,220

*In this figure are included, 127,086 tons, for the commerce with England, and 8,587 tons for that with France.

†The information concerning Exports, Imports and Tonnage which will be given in the course of this Chapter, is the same which was furnished to Professor J. E. Nourse, by M. F. A. Walker, Chief of the Statistical Bureau, United States Treasury Department, for his *Memoir on the Maritime Canal of Suez*, published, Washington City, 1870.

This reduction would give us a marked advantage in competition with the maritime powers of Europe.

In order to complete the enumeration of the advantages offered to our agricultural industry, and of the benefits to be derived by our shipping and commercial interests, in their relations with other countries situated upon our continent, we have to mention our trade with Mexico and Central America, of which we suppose a fourth part will make use of the interoceanic canal by reason of their geographical position:

Commerce with.	Valuation in 1869.	Tonnage in 1868. Tons.
Mexico,	$11,999,914	157,860
Central America,	4,219,656	82,040
Total	$16,219,570	239,900
One fourth of the sum total,	$4,054,892	59,975

Let us now consider the effect of an interoceanic canal upon our commerce with ports other than those of our own continent. The following table will show it in part:

Commerce with.	Valuation of Imports and Exports in 1869.	Tonnage in 1868. Tons.
The Sandwich islands,	$2,083,484	56,603
British Australia and New Zealand,	809,037	44,624
Asia,	25,584,853	107,884
	$28,477,374	209,111
Deducting that part of this tonnage which is direct with our Pacific ports, estimated		49,111
Remaining tonnage, belonging to the Atlantic Ports of the United States,*		160,000

The following table shows the comparative distances for the voyage from New York to the Sandwich islands, Austra-

* These figures are corroborated by the fact that, in 1868, forty-five vessels, with a register of 42,499 tons, cleared from the Atlantic ports for Japan and China.

lia, Japan and China, by way of the Cape and of an interoceanic canal :*

From New York to.	By way of Cape Horn.	By way of a canal at Tehuantepec.	In favor of an interoceanic Canal. Naut. miles.
Honolulu,	14,100	5,955	8,145
Melbourne,	12,720	9,600	3,120
Yokohama,	17,340	9,435	7,905
Shanghai,	18,300	10,355	7,945
Hong Kong,	19,000	10,755	8,245

The whale fishery is an important branch of our national industry, though to-day comparatively reduced from the proportions which it presented twenty-five years ago. This depression has been occasioned, among other causes, by the reduced value of oil, since it has been replaced in the consumption by other articles of lower prices. From this has arisen the necessity of reducing the selling price of the product of the fisheries in order to obtain a market for them, but who knows if, should the means of economizing the expenses of the Pacific fishery be offered, this industry would not be speedily restored to its old importance. We give below the returns of our whale fishery at different dates:

	Bbls. Sperm.	BBls. Whale Oil.	Bone, lbs.
1840,	157,761	207,908	2,000,000
1850,	92,892	200,608	2,869,200
1860,	73,708	140,805	1,337,650
1869,	47,936	85,011	603,603

The whaling fleet was made up in the following manner:

	Ships & Barks.	Brigs.	Schooners.	Tonnage. Tons.
1850,	581	21	12	196,110
1860,	508	19	42	176,842
1869,	218	22	81	73,137

*It may be interesting to know the distances from New York to the same ports by way of Suez:

To Melbourne	13,357 miles.
" Yokohoma,	13,493 "
" Shanghai,	12,458 "
" Hong Kong,	11,658 "

(From the Hydrographic Office of the Bureau of Navigation, Navy Department, Washington.)

An apparent difference of 103,705 tons results from this table between 1860 and 1870; but owing to loss by remeasurement the actual loss in tonnage is 93,095, showing in the last ten years a decrease of 55 per cent.

The American ships employed in the Pacific fisheries, and the average quantity of oil obtained by them at different dates, are shown by the following table:

	Number of ships.	Bbls. Sperm.	Bbls. Whale Oil.
1855,	217	878	189,579
1860,	121	518	62,678
1865,	59	617	36,415
1869,	43	890	38,275

The cost of outfit for this fleet is about $25,000 per vessel; the average length of a voyage is three years, of which one third is lost in going to and returning from the whaling grounds, lying in port to re-cooper, refit, &c., leaving but two years of actual fishing, or eight months in twelve. The rate of insurance upon vessels and outfits is three per cent. per annum, and the interest upon money invested in ships and outfits, which make no return until the end of the voyage, is six per cent. The loss by leakage is five per cent. during the voyage.

If this oil, then, instead of remaining on board of the vessels, or in depot at the Sandwich islands one or two years (for that which is taken the first year, remains on board two years, or in storage at some point in the Pacific, and that which is taken the second, one year) as dead capital, could be sent home across the isthmus canal, the gains would be great, for there would be a saving of both time and substance; the leakage would amount to but one per cent. instead of five; half the time, at least, which is now employed in consequence of having the ships to cooper, refit and refresh would be saved; the whaling year might be made to consist of ten instead of eight months, with, of course, a proportional increase of profits on the original outlay for additional two months of fishing; the vessels employed in the business, instead of being large ships capable of holding 2,800 barrels,—the proceeds of three years—would be only small ships capable of holding only one year's gathering; and the cost of smaller vessels, say one-third the size of those now employed, instead of running up to $25,000 cash for vessel and outfit, would by liberal estimate be brought down within less than half of that sum. The whale fishing industry touches at the same time the ship building interest and the fishing interest, properly so called, and its progress would do as much for the one as for the other.

Recapitulation of American shipping and trade, interested in in the construction of a Ship Canal across this continent.

	Annual tonnage. Tons.
Internal trade between the Pacific states and the Atlantic states,..............	500,000
Commerce between California and Europe,	200,000
" " " " the Atports of South America,............	7,977
Commerce of our Atlantic ports with Chili,	49,078
" " " " " Peru,	78,429
" " " " " the western coast of Mexico and Central America,.........................	59,975
Commerce of our Atlantic ports with the Sandwich islands, British Australia, New Zealand and Asia,.............	160,000
Pacific Whaling fishery, (one-third of our whole whaling Fleet,)	24,376
Total......................	1,079,835

Independently of this commercial movement and development, the European trade will contribute its share to the business of the canal. Besides those sailing vessels which would prefer to take this route on their voyage to Asia, the number of which it may be difficult to estimate, the commerce of Europe will employ the canal for its trade with the western coast of the American continent. We give here the statistics of this trade:

Table of the tonnage of European commerce with the western coast of America, south of California:

Countries.	England, 1867. Tons.	France, 1865. Tons.	Total of tonnage. Tons.
Chili,	220,771	25,263	246,034
Peru,	209,801	49,201	259,002
Ecuador,	2,725	2,283	5,008
One-fourth of the whole tonnage (for the western coast) of			
Mexico,	11,200	17,336	28,536
Central America,	3,825	5,360	9,185
New Granada,	5,509	3,350	8,859
Total,	453,831	102,793	556,624
Add: one-fourth of the above as the estimated tonnage for all other European nations, besides England and France,			139,156
Total,			695,780

COMPARISON BETWEEN THE NORTHERN AND SOUTHERN EXTREMITIES OF THE AMERICAN ISTHMUS, WITH REFERENCE TO THE LOCATION OF A SHIP CANAL.

We are all aware that the central part of our continent, which we call the Isthmus, extends from Tehuantepec to the main-land of South America with a length of about fifteen hundred miles.

If we imagine two canals, one at each extremity of this isthmus, it is not strictly true that in making a voyage from a northeastern latitude to one corresponding on the Northwest,and by taking the southern canal instead of the northern, we should add twice the length of the Isthmus, or three thousand miles, to our voyage. Owing to the configuration of the continent, south of Cape Hatteras, and the location of the Antilles and their neighboring shoals, the navigator from the

Northeast—at the Atlantic side—is compelled to approach the Isthmus in an oblique direction; he does not coast it from north to south. On the Pacific side the case is different; there the sailor, going from north to south or from south to north, skirts the shores of Central America, and describes in his course a distance corresponding nearly to the length of the Isthmus. For these reasons a difference of from fifteen hundred to two thousand miles is all that is admitted in a voyage from New York to San Francisco, in favor of the northern route. This difference, however, remains sufficiently formidable in a voyage of about five thousand miles, supposing the existence of an interoceanic canal. For steam navigation the difference is naturally somewhat less.

In the table which we have given in the first Chapter, the difference in a voyage to San Francisco, between the two routes of Panama and Tehuantepec, is estimated at 1,477 statute miles from New York, and 1,131 from Europe in favor of the latter. Panama is not precisely the southern extremity of the Isthmus. Darien, for instance, which is now being discussed with reference to a ship canal, is situated still further to the South. It would, therefore, be necessary to increase these figures proportionally in making estimates for that route. Nevertheless the tables furnished lately by the Bureau of Navigation of the Department of Navy, at Washington, and which we will quote afterwards, indicate for Darien a still lower figure for steam navigation. We are able to explain this only by the remark given in these tables, that the distances are merely *estimated* for those sections of the route on which there are no established steam lines. In the subject which we have now under discussion, the interests of the sailing marine have all their own importance, as a great part of the commerce between the Atlantic and Pacific states, especially by reason of the nature of their cargoes, will be carried on by preference in sailing vessels. The difference in the distance to be run by the one route or the other has thus to be taken here into account at its full value.

It is easy to estimate by the foregoing statistical tables

the traffic which would go by way of the American canal, and especially that which relates to our own continent. We have seen that in this latter category, which supplies the larger part of the tonnage indicated—as it amounts to 1,079,835 tons—half of it goes from the Northwest to the Northeast of our continent, and the reverse, and one-fifth from the Northwest of America to the Northwest of Europe, and reciprocally. Should we offer to impose upon 700,000 tons out of the million—or upon three-fourths of our whole commercial movement—an unnecessary detour of 1,500 miles, by forcing it to cross at the southern rather than the northern end of the Isthmus? Certainly no one would have the courage to advocate such a proposition. The location of a ship canal at Darien wonld bring about precisely this most singular achievement.

At first thought, that which we have just said will stagger the notions popularly entertained concerning an American canal, but two leading ideas develop themselves at once on a serious examination of the question. The first is that the American canal is destined to serve especially the commercial interests of America, as will at once appear from the tables which we have given, showing that out of a commerce of about eighteen hundred thousand tons which is interested in the construction of the canal, that of America stands for about one million. The second point which becomes apparent is that, in providing first for the interests of American commerce in the location of the canal, those of all other parties are at the same time equally protected.

To render still more striking the effect of the location of the interoceanic canal at one point rather than the other, let us compare the results which would be attained by the two rival routes. For this purpose we give here tabular statements, prepared in the Hydrographic Office of the Bureau of Navigation, indicating the distances from New York and New Orleans to the principal ports concerned by way of a canal at Darien and of one at Tehuantepec. These tables give at the same time the distances *via* Cape Horn.

*Table of distances from New York :**

To	*via* Cape Horn.	*via* Isthmus of Darien.	*via* Isthmus of Tehuantepec.	In favor of the canal at Tehuantepec. Naut. miles.
San Francisco,..	14,200	5,300	4,400	900
Mazatlan,......	13,000	4,060	3,135	925
Melbourne,.....	12,720	9,890	9,600	290
Honolulu,......	14,100	6,730	5,955	775
Yokohama,.....	17,340	10,210	9,435	775
Shanghai,......	18,300	11,100	10,355	745
Hong Kong,....	19,000	11,500	10,755	745

*Table of distances from New Orleans :**

To	*via* Cape Horn.	*via* Isthmus of Darien.	*via* Isthmus of Tehuantepec.	In favor of the canal at Tehuantepec. Naut. miles.
San Francisco,..	14,500	4,650	3,070	1,580
Mazatlan,.......	13,300	3,390	1,800	1,590
Melbourne,.....	13,000	9,250	8,260	990
Honolulu,......	14,400	6,030	4,620	1,410
Yokohama,......	17,600	9,510	8,100	1,410
Shanghai,.......	22,300	10,430	9,020	1,410
Hong Kong,....	19,300	10,830	9,400	1,430

We have already seen that the distance from the Lezard to San Francisco is *via* Cape Horn 13,624, by way of Panama 7,502 and by way of Tehuantepec 6,671; difference in favor of the latter direction of 971 nautical miles, which is to be increased with reference to the more southerly locality of Darien. We give now the respective distances from the Lezard to the prominent ports of eastern Asia by way of a canal at Darien and of one at Tehuantepec.

Distances from Liverpool to East Asia :

To	*via* Isthmus of Darien.	*via* Isthmus of Tehuantepec.	In favor of the canal at Tehuantepec. Naut. miles.
Yokohama,..................	12,900	12,400	500
Shanghai,....................	13,820	13,320	500
Hong Kong,................	14,220	13,720	500

*" *In general the distances are measured on steam routes, when lines are established, and are approximately correct.*"—Observation by the Hydrographic Office to its tables.

The Asiatico-European traffic through the American canal would certainly be inferior in amount to the trade which, according to our tables, is directly interested in the construction of the proposed transit, and to whose especial convenience the canal should be adapted. In case the selection made of the location of the canal should not answer completely the requirements of foreign commerce, we could not hesitate on that account, as our own interests must first of all be protected; but when it is shown that the northern location gives not only an advantage to American commerce, but to that of Europe also, we can but be the more strongly confirmed in our choice.

In commerce, all questions become affairs of arithmetic and everything finally must be reduced to figures. Without attempting in any case to make too elaborate an argument, let us calculate the loss to American commerce, which would be caused by the adoption of the Darien route. We see by the calculation made, in the course of this Chapter, of the expenses of a ship of a thousand tons, from New York to San Francisco, by way of the Cape and by way of the canal, that the latter are estimated at $6,843, for ship and and cargo. If, in consequence of a detour occasioned by the location at Darien, this voyage of about 5,000 miles should be increased by 1,500, the cost of transportation, which is nearly in exact proportion to the duration of the voyage, would be augmented by at least one-fourth, say $1,710. This is for the commerce between New York and San Francisco amounting to 500,000 tons, and if we represent this movement by five hundred vessels, averaging one thousand tons each, we find that the annual augmentation in the cost of transportation would be $855,000, on account of the unnecessary detour. The shipping between California and Europe amounts annually to 200,000 tons. We have seen that for the trade of Europe with California the detour occasioned by a canal on the southern part of the Isthmus, if it is not 1,500, is at least 1,000 miles. We adopt, therefore, to represent the cost of the detour to this branch of trade, one-fifth of the $6,843, mentioned above for the cost of a voyage of a sailing vessel over five thousand miles, say $1,368, and allowing for the given commercial movement of 200,000 tons two hundred ships of one thousand tons average, we see that the increase of expenses would be $273,600. Adding this to the $855,000, we have the sum of $1,128,600 for the loss which the location of a canal in the southern part of the Isthmus would cause annually to our commerce, without taking into account the loss to our Asiatic and other shipping, and the impossibility of bringing our Pacific fisheries as near as is desirable to their ports of outfit.

Two other points, relating to the highest questions of humanity and good policy, ought not to be permitted to escape our attention in treating of the comparative advantages of the northern and southern parts of the American isthmus with reference to the present subject.

We are all aware of the evil reputation of the climate of the southern part of the Isthmus. This ill repute dates from a very early day, for we can quote from the account of a voyage made in 1535 by Don Alonzo de Guzman Henriquez, republished by the "Hakluyt Society" in London 1862, the following passage: "On my arrival at the port of Nombre de Dios, in the province of Castilla del Oro (the southern end of the American isthmus), I learned that the native name of the place means *Bones*, and was so called on account of the number of people who have died there." Taking this quotation for what it is worth, it is however certain that even to this day Panama and Darien have not been able to free themselves from an evil fame on account of climate. A bad and dangerous climate is in itself a great inconvenience for a country, but it becomes a veritable obstacle when the undertaking of an interoceanic canal is to be executed under such unfavorable conditions, and when a great highway of the world is to be surrounded by such a peril. From this point of view the southern part of the Isthmus lacks the requisite qualities.

The entrance to the Caribbean sea, which washes the shores of the southern isthmus, is commanded by English cannon. What would become of our access to our canal in time of war, located as it would be in a situation where its defence by us would be difficult, if not impossible? International wars become more and more unfrequent, as commercial and industrial development establishes between the different peoples that community of material interests which is of itself the surest guaranty of peace; but if such a calamity should come, here again the extreme north of the Isthmus offers us special advantages. A canal terminating in the gulf of Mexico would be very easily protected in time of war, and by making in case of need the Gulf a *mare clausum*, our merchant marine would be secure from all attack, and our relations with the Pacific could be sustained without any interruption. This is a consideration which, in the eyes of our statesmen, ought to constitute an argument in favor of the more northerly locality.

CHAPTER FOURTH.

Ship Canal Project. The most advantageous Location, with Reference to the Interests of the United States.

From that which is contained in the preceding Chapters we may deduce two leading facts.

The first is that the execution of a "thorough cut" across the narrower part of the American isthmus cannot probably be accomplished without the expenditure of a sum out of all proportion with the revenue which the work would be likely to return for the capital employed. The second fact has reference to the use which it is expected that the people of the United States would make of the new means of communication projected, and which requires that its location should be as near as possible to their own frontiers, the best locality being on the gulf of Mexico and traversing the Isthmus at a point, where it is wider than at the southern extremity, and where a system of locks would be necessary.

This state of the question carries us back to a project which was conceived more than twenty-five years ago, and which failed of execution, only because the course of events at that time was not propitious. We refer to the survey made by G. Moro, in 1842, with a view to utilize the isthmus of Tehuantepec for the construction of a canal in connection with the river Goatzacoalcos. At that time it was Europe, that more particularly busied itself with the project of penetrating the American isthmus, with the view of facilitating its trade with the Indies. England and France had made explorations for that purpose at Darien and at Panama. The selection of the narrowest part of the Isthmus for the first explorations, for a route for a ship canal, sufficiently explains itself. To-day, when the interests of America have been developed to so high a point; when the need, which led the powers mentioned to examine the American isthmus, has been in great part satisfied by the opening of the Suez canal, the whole face of the question is changed. The location of a canal to traverse the American isthmus must now be decided with reference to the accommodation of our own continent, and the penetration of our "narrow lands" takes the form of an enterprise whose accomplishment affects American interests peculiarly.

In a volume which we published in 1847, designed to represent to Europe the prodigious development of artificial means of communication in the United States, at a time when the old world seemed to be awakening from a species of lethargy, we remarked that each step in the world's progress has its especial epoch assigned for its attainment. "There are yet works which are reserved to be accomplished by the progressive march of our civilization. There are innovations which become successes, because the age in which they make their appearance is adapted to their practical application, and the realization of which is only possible because the population, which is to receive the benefit of them, finds itself in a certain requisite condition."

Thus it is with the project of a canal to traverse the isthmus of Tehuantepec. Set on foot in 1843, although received with favor, it did not arouse sufficient interest to secure its accomplishment. To-day, when in another hemisphere a canal has been opened between two oceans; when the subject of a canal to traverse the American isthmus is being seriously agitated; when projects for a thorough cut in the southern portion of the Isthmus are presented, as if to invite us to a discussion and to show the superior advantages of a canal at Tehuantepec, the time has come to revive the past, and to bring the project of 1843 once more before the public, with a view to its execution.

If it was necessary to show the priority which antiquity gives in favor of the Tehuantepec route in the search for a navigable way between the two seas, it would be easy to establish such a preference; but there are more important considerations to attract our attention to that line. However that may be, it is from this point that we have accounts of the earliest explorations made to find the means of joining the two seas by inland navigation. Hernan Cortez, in his fourth letter to Charles V., makes mention of an expedition despatched for this purpose in the direction of Guatemala, "because," he says, "the opinion of many pilots is that in that region there exists an easy passage from sea to sea, a thing, which I have the greatest desire in the world to find for the great advantage which, in my opinion, your Majesty would derive from it."* The expedition, as we know, was not only limited to the gulf of Honduras; they ascended also the Goatzacoalcos and its tributaries, which river, after having traversed the greater part of the barrier between the Atlantic and Pacific, flows into the gulf of Mexico. The result of the soundings made at that time has been handed down to our own day. It is said, in the despatch of Cortez to the Emperor: "They found two fathoms and half of water in its entrance, in the shallowest part, and ascending twelve leagues the least they found was five and six fathoms." These soundings were made in 1520, and give about the same depth over the bar at the mouth of the Goatzacoalcos which is now found.

Since the time when Balboa, an explorer of the isthmus of Panama, first discovered the Pacific, the navigators of that age did not cease to search at different points on the coast for the means of penetrating the continent, in order to shorten the voyage between Europe and Asia. Other enterprising men, their contemporaries, dreamed of the junction of the two oceans by means of artificial water communication

---

*"---- como porque hay opinion de muchos pilotes que por aquella bahia sale estrecho al otro mar, que es la cosa que yo, en este mundo, mas deseo topar por el gran servicio que se me presenta que de ella Vuestra cesárea Majestad recibiria."—*Original Text.*

across the central parts of America, but, at the very moment when it was established that nature herself had not provided the desired transit, and that art must therefore supply it, the Spanish government decided to hand down to another age the solution of the problem. It was only two and a half centuries later, in 1774, that Spain, adopting a more liberal policy, once more sought for an interoceanic passage, by way of the isthmus of Tehuantepec. By order of the Viceroy Antonio Bucareli, Don Augustin Cramer, (Teniente del Rey), commander of the castle of San Juan de Ulua, was charged with the exploration of that isthmus.

His report commences with this important notice:

"The bar of the river Goatzaeoalcos has on it, at half-tide, 25 Palms (6 yards) of water excepting a very small portion of its length, on which there are only 18 Palms. These soundings correspond with those taken on the first survey and afterwards by me; for which reason, and as frequent soundings taken by the present pilots during the last thirteen years agree with them, it may be inferred, that the said bar is permanently in the same state, or that, if any variation occurs, it is so inconsiderable that it has escaped notice. After passing the bar the river is six to eight fathoms deep."

Cramer continues his narrative, briefly describing, but with admirable exactness, the course of the river up to Mal Paso, and demonstrates the facilities which the country presents for making a good road from this point to Tehuantepec, concluding with the remarkable observations here literally transcribed.

"The river courses with the mountain chain, interrupted between Santa Maria Petapa, and San Miguel Chimalapa, and the evenness of the grounds plainly indicate that it would not be a work of great difficulty, nor excessively costly, to effect a communication between the two seas across this isthmus. In the supposition that the waters of the rivers Almaloya and Citune were held back, a canal might be opened to join them with those of the San Miguel or Chicapa, the course of which into the Pacific ocean by the bar of San Francisco passes by the Venta de Chicapa, and from this spot forwards there are no further difficulties, because it is one perfect plain as far as Tehuantepec."

An examination of the topography of the Isthmus will show how rational was this project, bearing in mind its application to a canal of small dimensions, such as was contemplated by Don Cramer. It was with reference to these results, that Humboldt, after having very properly asserted that until his time "the topography of the isthmus of Tehuantepec was quite unknown in Europe," adds "we cannot but doubt, that this point of the globe deserves no less attention than the lake of Nicaragua."

The political events which followed prevented the accomplishment of the purposes of the Spanish government, and it was not until 1842 that the question was again revived, when Don José de Garay, proposed to the government of the Republic of Mexico, to undertake the construction of a line of communication across Tehuantepec. Article 2d, of the Act of concession, granted to Sr. de Garay by President Santa Anna, March 1st 1842, provides: "The line of communication shall be performed by water, but when this may not be convenient, then a railroad and steam carriages may be used." The grantee caused the exploration of the isthmus, with a view to the construction of a canal, and it is the survey made at that time to which we would now call the attention of the public.

Two principal fractions distinguish the topography of the isthmus of Tehuantepec. The first, is the marked depression in the chain of the Cordilleras at that point, precisely where the continent is the narrowest, as if nature herself had desired to prepare facilities for a passage from sea to sea. The second, is the number of considerable rivers draining the slopes of the mountains on either side, and of which the most important is the Goatzacoalcos with its tributaries. Another remarkable circumstance is that the courses of the rivers, in general, are adapted in a marvellous degree to the formation of a water way across the isthmus, and that at the summit of the mountainous region, where the waters are divided to flow down on either slope, there exists a sufficient supply of water to feed the summit level of a canal.

Mr. G. Moro, entrusted by Mr. de Garay with the examination of these several characteristics of the isthmus, has availed himself of them with much intelligence, if we are to judge by his reported project. Before, however, we say more upon these points, we will describe, following the text of the original report of Mr. Moro, the topography and geography of that part of the isthmus, which is more particularly treated of with reference to the subject before us.

TOPOGRAPHY OF THE SOUTHERN PART OF THE ISTHMUS.

All accounts agree as to the facility with which the river Goatzacoalcos might be rendered navigable at least so far as its confluence with the Sarabia; therefore the space which it was the most important to explore was that intervening between this confluence and the shores of the Pacific.

COAST OF THE PACIFIC AND LAGOONS.

It has been suggested that the bay of Ventosa might be used for the purpose of port for the future canal, but on examination it was found that its small size, as even supposing that it were deep enough, makes it not very fit for such purpose without necessitating artificial works.*

Mr. Moro visited the two lakes, situated along side the Pacific, west of Ventosa. A surveying party sailed from the quai of Salina, near the Estacada, and passing between the islands of Monapos-tiac and Natar-tiac, arrived at San Dionisio, the sounding line constantly showing nearly six meters, (twenty feet) depth of water, the bottom being mud and shingle, both easy to remove. On proceeding thither,

* It is true that Cortez launched a few vessels in that cove, but it is well known that in those times vessels were built of small dimensions, and probably he made use of that spot, not because he considered it fit and safe for such an operation, but simply because it was the only one near at hand where it could be at all accomplished.

the eastern part of the lower lagoon attracted Mr. Moro's attention, as its vicinity to the Boca Barra and the canal of Santa Teresa, its considerable depth, the excellent bottom, and the circumstance of being so well sheltered from the prevailing winds, fitted it admirably for a commodious and safe anchorage. It was surveyed and the Boca Barra was explored. The tide was too strong to use the sounding line, but it was evident that a sand bank obstructs *internally* the Boca Barra throughout its whole length from east to west.

As the idea, that a canal of great dimensions was the only advantageous means of effecting the desired communication, every endeavor was made to ascertain the course and volume of the waters of the several rivers in this part of the isthmus. Amongst them all, particular attention was directed to the river Ostuta, remarkable for the volume and regular course of its waters, which, after having formed the lagoon situated in the neighborhood of San Francisco, flow through the Barilla and the mouth of Lagartero in the Duicnahuanot (lake inferior). On entering the eastern lagoon the currents of the Ostuta flow along the southern shore, and, decreasing gradually in their impetus, they reach the Boca Barra so powerless as to deposit there the sands they bring with them; these are afterwards shaped into a large bank by the waves, kept in incessant agitation by the northerly wind which prevails almost constantly in those regions.

In the project which will be proposed, it is calculated to make use of the waters of the Ostuta, taken from the "sierra" in order to feed the canal, by doing which, the principal cause of the formation of this bank would be removed. The sand bank of the Boca Barra, however, may be attributed to another and more powerful cause. The river Tehuantepec flowed, not many years ago, into the western lower lagoon. The opposing currents of both rivers destroyed reciprocally their strength, and caused the deposit in that particular spot of the matter they bring with them.

Taking advantage of a calm between two tides, a party succeeded in going out to sea through the Boca Barra and executing the soundings indicated in the map. They found that, immediately after passing the bank, there is a channel the depth of which, even in the shallowest part, is of nearly nineteen and three-fourth feet, this depth increasing afterwards rapidly. Mr. Moro now proceeded northward, passing through Chivela to

GUICHICOVI

which is situated at the commencement of the rugged part of the "sierra," The gentle hills in the neighborhood of Chivela, approaching this spot, are, at intervals, interrupted by precipitous ravines, through which several rivers and streams find a passage for their waters. The surface of the ground becomes more level, receding from Guichicovi towards Boca de Monte, from whence, as far as the Mal Paso, it finally becomes a perfect plain occupied by a forrest of useful and precious timber. On arriving at the Mal Paso, they were surprised at the view presented by the Goatzacoalcos, which from the transparency and slow progress of its waters had more the appearance of an artificial canal than that of a mighty river. Its banks of strong clay are firm and easy of access, with an almost uniform elevation of eight or twelve feet, which leads to the supposition that the river runs along a level surface, although the thick woods, which line its shores, conceal from view the topographical aspect of the land covered by them.

TABLE LAND OF TARIFA.

After having returned to Chivela, the surveying party proceeded northwest, towards Tarifa, along a table land covered with a great number of gentle and interrupted declivities, and along a road so level, that it inspired Mr. Moro with the most flattering hopes. From Tarifa the ground continues to be still more favorable as far as the Portillo, or gap, from which a rapid descent leads to the plain, in which is situated the Venta de Chicapa. During that time operations had actively continued, not only in the lower part of the country, but also in that which extends from the village of San Miguel to the hills of Petapa. The ground from San Miguel to the river del Corte,* in the neighborhood of Santa Maria Chimalapa, was likewise examined.

Mr. Moro now resolved to reconnoitre the points which had been fixed during his absence. On arriving at one of these, on the summit of a hill, about one mile to the North of the village of San Miguel, and which afterwards received in commemoration the name of Cerro de Albricias, (Reward Hill), he saw the problem at once solved. The Sierra Madre (or principal chain of the Andes) appears to be interrupted, as the engineer Cramer judiciously observed, between Santa Maria Petapa and San Miguel Chimalapa. On the western side it descends rapidly, as far as the first of these villages, and proceeds again suddenly towards the East of the second, leaving in the middle a surface comparatively level. To the South the small chain of Masahua and Espinosa, of moderate elevation, forms a barrier between this hilly tract of ground and the true plain, terminating at their extremities in two openings, or gaps, through the westernmost of which descends the road from Chevila, leading to the plain, and another through the eastern from Tarifa to the Venta de Chicapa. On the North, the table-land extends itself gently, descending as far as the Goatzacoalcos and from thence to the Atlantic.

THE RIVER CHICAPA

reaches San Miguel, occupying in its course from east to west the bottom of a straight dale, between two uninterrupted chains of mountains, and then suddenly turns in a southerly direction towards the plain, wherein is the upper lagoon which receives its waters. Running in a line diametrically opposite to the first course of the Chicapa, namely, from west to east, the stream of Monetza joins the above river

---

* This part of the Goatzacoalcos is still called the river *del Corte*, because it flows through the country, where the timber for ship building was cut by the Spanish government, to be sent to Havana.

near San Miguel, by another dale, which in reality is only the continuation of the first, and would lead directly to Tarifa, were it not divided from the plain, on which this estate lies, by a small chain of which the Cerro del Convento forms a part. The village of San Miguel is situated in a small valley, lower than the plain of Tarifa by more than two hundred and sixty-four feet; but as the most northern of the two chains between which the Chicapa and Monetza are enclosed, has no interruption whatever, it was thought it possible to convey along its side the waters of the Chicapa as far as Tarifa, from whence they might be distributed to both seas; neither was it considered difficult to surmount the natural barrier formed by the small chain of Convento, between the valley of the Monetza and the table-land of Tarifa. From San Miguel to the Ultimo Rancho five constant streams join the Chicapa, and the surveying party having measured the waters of this river in a point below its junction with these streams, found them equivalent to more than five meters, or one hundred and seventy-six cubic feet, per second; so that by adding to it the Monetza and the stream which runs through San Miguel, called Xoxocuta, a body of waters of about seven cubic meters, or two hundred and forty-seven cubic feet, may be reckoned upon. According to all the information collected, these waters were then in a state which might be considered the *minimum* of their quantity, and they are always exceedingly clear and pure.

A barometrical level, obtained from observations performed simultaneously at Tarifa and at the source of the Monetza, showed that the level of the latter is nearly the same than that of the stream adjoining Tarifa, the waters of which run to the Goatzacoalcos, as a confluent of the Malatengo. The ground which lies between Tarifa, and the source of Monetza, although level, is now and then intersected by torrent streams, the waters of which flow into the Monetza; and as these streams have their origin at a short distance from Tarifa, this according to Mr. Moro, ought to be considered as the proper spot for the division of the waters in the canal.

The houses of Tarifa are somewhat elevated, in the midst

of a ground so level, that in the rainy season it becomes inundated, for which reason this plain has been called the *lake* of Tarifa. Mr. Moro took advantage of this circumstance to save the trouble of a new levelling between the latter place and the Portillo, or opening of the road to the Venta, since the line left by the waters on subsiding clearly shows that the two points are nearly on a level, thus, with a cut a foot or so deep in the edge of the Portillo, the waters to the South of Tarifa would proceed toward the Pacific, whilst those on the northern side naturally run towards the other sea.

All that now was wanting, was to find the manner of increasing the volume of available waters, and to avoid having recourse to the expensive means of constructing great reservoirs.

The waters of the Almoloya, Citune and other streams on the side of the Chivela were calculated, but their distance from Tarifa and the difficulties of the ground, they would have to cross, would make their conveyance somewhat expensive; and therefore

THE RIVER OSTUTA

was examined. At Zanatepec the surveying party experienced some difficulty in fording the river, which was rather swollen, notwithstanding which its waters continued to be perfectly clear as far as that spot. The documents deposited in the archives of the village were examined, amongst which a few fragments of a map of the land comprised in its jurisdiction was discovered, and that which most particularly attracted attention, was to find, noted down in this document, the traditional opinion that the river Ostuta takes its source in a lake. After several vain attempts, the party succeeded, by following up the banks of the river, in reaching the foot of the high hills, from whence it proceeds. Throughout the whole distance the river receives no constant tributary, and its waters increase as they approach their source, which shows that a portion of them becomes absorbed in the lower part of the course of the river. The waters of the

Ostuta were not measured, not only on account of the difficulty of doing so, but because they often vary in an extraordinary manner; but, according to Mr. Moro's opinion, it may be asserted that they are never less than three times as copious as those of the Chicapa, and frequently more than six.

The wild state of the country prevented Mr. Moro from discovering the adjacent grounds; but the direction in which he had gone made him suppose that he was near the upper course of the Chicapa. The elevated situation in which he was, and the proximity of the two rivers, seemed to promise that there would be no great difficulty in effecting their junction; but the intervening woods, by concealing from view the topographical aspect of the ground, did not permit a fair estimate being formed of the difficulties there might be to encounter. The river came down precipitously from the mountains and, for a considerable distance, had ceased to be fordable. It was every moment more and more difficult to ascend its course along the same bank, and at last it became evident that, in order to estimate correctly the obstacles which might oppose themselves to the projected junction, nothing else remained, but to reach, if possible, the very spot where he then was, by descending along the craggy side of the Cerro Atravesado which lay opposite.

FACILITY OF JOINING THE WATERS OF OSTUTA AND CHICAPA TOGETHER.

Meanwhile it appeared evident that both, the Chicapa and Ostuta, proceed from that portion of these territories, where the Sierra Madre is highest; which explains why these rivers increase and diminish simultaneously without its being at all necessary to suppose that they owe their origin to a lake. On his return from this expedition up the Ostuta Mr. Moro went to Niltepec and ascended the Atravesado. The Cerro Atravesado stands completely isolated on every side, except here, where it ends in a kind of ridge, and which descending to the valley is joined by another, proceeding from the summit of the Sierra Madre. Resolving to follow the first of these ridges, in order to explore the ground which divides the two rivers, he was not long in reaching the point where it is most depressed, and from which the relative position of both rivers was perfectly clear and obvious. Near to the West was the deep ravine through which the Chicapa runs, and to the East the elevated grounds of the bed of the Ostuta, which had just been visited and which he recognized perfectly at a distance of less than a league. The difference of level between those two points is so considerable, that there cannot be a doubt of the facility of effecting the junction of the two rivers; and it is no less evident that in the short space which intervenes, there is no obstacle whatever to prevent it. The weather clearing up, he was enabled to make several observations from points still more elevated, by means of which he ascertained beyond all question the favorable nature of the ground, and no doubt remained in his mind on the subject.

At the same time Mr. Moro undertook to explore the country between Tarifa and the confluence of the Malatengo and del Corte (Goatzacoalcos). This part of the country is the most fertile and pleasant that it is possible to imagine. The plains near the rivers, cultivated by the inhabitants of Bario, Santa Maria Petapa and San Juan Guichicovi, give an idea of the astonishing fertility of the soil since the natives only come in time to burn down the brushwood and sow without cultivation, scarcely ever visiting their cornfields until the harvest time. The principal object in this later survey was to find out the best line through which a canal might be opened from Tarifa to the Goatzacoalcos. From Tarifa the waters descend naturally to this mighty river through grounds by no means too rugged, whilst the very existence of a labyrinth of hillocks, almost all individually isolated, or else joined together by ridges of an insignificant thickness, is sufficient to prove the practicability of the work, but most probably presenting numerous solutions of the problem.

DESCRIPTION OF THE RIVER GOATZACOALCOS AND ITS AFFLUENTS.

The river Goatzacoalcos* takes its rise in the unexplored part of the Sierra Madre, and flows into the gulf of Mexico, in 18° 8′ 30″ north latitude and 94° 17′ west longitude from Greenwich.

The Chimalapilla falls into the Goatzacoalcos, on its right bank four and a half miles to the S. S. E. of the village of Santa Maria Chimalapa, and its confluence is three hundred and ninty-three feet above the level of the sea. As far as the confluence with the river del Milagro, which enters on the left bank at one and one-half miles to the W. N. W. of Santa Maria, the Goatzacoalcos takes a precipitous course through a deep ravine, with a descent of one hundred and thirty-two feet in the space of twelve miles. The volume of water now filling the river is considerable, for as Mr. Moro descended, he found it to be about fifty-seven cubic yards per second, and the Indians assured him that it was rarely less.

Beyond the confluence of the Milagro, the river, hitherto running from east to west, follows a general direction towards the S. W. as far as the mouth of the Escolapa, and after that to the N. W. as far as that of the Malatengo. Both these rivers flow into the Goatzacoalcos by its left bank. The Escolapa as well as the Milagro, and the streams which unite with it, have their sources in the desert part of the Sierra to the east of the road which leads from San Miguel to Santa Maria Chimalapa. The course of the Malatengo and its tributaries are laid down upon the map.

---

* Many disputes have arisen with regard to the orthography of this name. In the despatches of Hernan Cortes to the Emperor Charles V., he writes it in no less than six different ways, viz: "*Mazamalco,*" "*Ouacalco,*" "*Cuicicacalco,*" "*Guazacualco,*" *and* "*Guazagualco.*" The veteran soldier Bernal Diaz del Castillo, who resided more than thirty years in the province, calls it "*Cuasualco,*" De Solis, on the other hand, writes it "*Goatzacoalcos,*" and the Abbé Clavigero, who, from his extensive knowledge of the languages of Mexico, is perhaps the best authority, writes it after this manner, viz: "*Coatzacualco.*" We have followed De Solis, as in accordance with the letter of the grant of the Tehuantepec railway and the prevailing custom of official papers at this date.

As the Malatengo is approached, the hills reappear with more elevation and frequency on the borders, and continue the same beyond its confluence. The accession of waters to the Goatzacoalcos is now more perceptible in its greater depth, which from this place to the mouth of the Sarabia is generally from five to eight and a half feet and sometimes even sixteen and a half feet, whilst in its breadth it does not exceed forty-four yards.

Next after the Malatengo the rivulet Chico joins on the right bank coming from the Sierra of Chimalapa; and at no great distance on the other side enters a stream, near which is an ancient wharf, called Mal Paso, so named on account of a strong rapid a little below it and which caused it to be abandoned. At the present day another loading place is called by the same name, but this is two hundred and twenty yards above the Paso del Sarabia, close to the mouth of the river of the same name. This rapid, which is the strongest to be found after leaving the Malatengo, is formed of various ridges of calcareous spar and granite, and occupies a space of two hundred yards. The first of these rocks frequently occurs at the base of the hills, and often forms smaller rapids.

After the junction of the Sarabia the hills become inconsiderable, and almost entirely disappear a little below the river Jumuapa (or de la Puerta); the rapids, also, are less frequent, and the last of them, called the Suchil, is seen just before reaching the mouth of the river Jaltepec (or de los Mijes).

The rivers Sarabia, Jumuapa, and Jaltepec enter the Goatzacoalcos on the left bank, and next to them the Chalchijapa on the right hand. The two first descend from the sierra of Santa Maria Guienagate.

Between the confluence of the Chalchijapa and the point of Horqueta, where the river is divided into two branches, the stream Colorado, the rivers Naranjo and Peñas Blancas, and the stream Cuapinoloya join the river by its left bank, and the brook Churriagao by the right; the latter and the Peñas Blancas come from large lagoons not far distant.

The general course of the Goatzacoalcos from the confluence of the Malatengo to that of the Jumuapa is from S. to N.; then it runs N. W. until it meets the Jaltepec; and thence to the bar its course is N. E. The length from the mouth of the Malatengo to the Sarabia is twenty-two miles; from the Sarabia to the Jumuapa, seventeen; from the Jumuapa to the Chalchijapa, twenty-two and a half; and to the Horqueta, forty and a half more, being a distance of one hundred and two miles, between the Malatengo and the Horqueta.

The banks of the river, after quitting the hills, are generally from ten to seventeen feet high, without being steep; yet they are sometimes so low as to be covered in times of flood. At some few spots called *cerritos* or hillocks, the banks are from forty to sixty-six feet high, and are composed of beds of clay.

In consequence of the low and sloping banks which here suffer the river to spread out laterally, and the slowness of the current, which after the confluence of the Jaltepec is scarcely apparent, the depth of the stream does not increase so much as might be expected; and during the dry season, shoals are even to be met with, covered only by twenty inches of water. These shoals are formed of sand and gravel, and almost all of them are small. Those of any extent are, one commencing below Tecolotepec, which occupies the greater part of the bend of Cascajal; another between the river Naranjo and the brook Churriagao; another that of Cuapinoloya between the island of this same name and one a little lower down; and lastly, that of Horqueta, obstructing the entrance of the two branches of the river which is divided at this point.

These two branches again unite after having formed the island of Tacamichapa. The one to the west called Mistan is longer and narrower than that to the east called Apotzongo; the length of the first is thirty-four miles, its width between one hundred and one hundred and ten yards, or about twenty to thirty yards less than the river was before it became divided; and the depth is about thirteen and a half feet. Several streams fall into it.

After the junction of the two branches, the Goatzacoalcos receives on its right the rivulet Ishuatepec, the stream of Otapa, and the river Coahuapa, the mouth of which is ten miles from the lower end of the island of Tacamichapa. The source of this river is unknown, and the district it traverses is a desert. The stream Otapa comes from some small lagoons producing salt in abundance.

Four miles and a half below the confluence of the Coahuapa, but on the opposite shore, is the village of Mina-titlan; and at four and a half more below this, the river Uspanapan joins the Goatzacoalcos by its right bank. Half way between the river Coahuapa and Mina-titlan is situated, on the left bank in front of an islet, the common entrance to the creeks Tacojalpa, Ojozapa, and Cuamecatan, in which the pine logs destined for the arsenal at Havanna were formerly deposited.

The Uspanapan is the most considerable of all the numerous tributaries of the Goatzacoalcos. At ten and a quarter miles below the Uspanapan, and five and a quarter from the bar, is found on the left the confluence with the river Tierra Nueva, or the Calzadas, this being the channel by which the Goatzacoalcos unites with the river Huasuntan which empties itself into the sea by the mouth of the Barrilla, not practicable for large vessels.

The banks of the river here are very low, and frequently flooded, and there are many creeks; the most remarkable of which are, that of Tacoteno, on the left bank below Paso Nuevo, which reaches back to near Mina-titlan, and that of Coatajapa on the right hand, which flows near the village of Yshuatlan.

The depth of the Goatzacoalcos, from the separation of the branches which form the island of Tacamichapa to the mouth of the Coahuapa, is twenty-six and a half feet, and from there to the bar not less than thirty-three to forty feet. Its breadth, where narrowest, is from one hundred and thirty to one hundred and seventy yards; and in some places below the mouth of Tierra Nueva it is nearly seven hundred and seventy yards. It will therefore be seen, that as far as the island of Tacamichapa, a distance of thirty-five miles, or at least up to the confluence of the Coahuapa, the Goatzacoalcos is navigable in all seasons and for every class of ships, forming a convenient as well as most secure harbor.*

IMPROVING THE NAVIGATION OF THE GOATZACOALCOS AND DREDGING A CANAL THROUGH THE LAGOONS ON THE PACIFIC.

The various plans which Mr. Moro has submitted are formed on the supposition of the Goatzacoalcos being rendered navigable as far as its confluence with the Malatengo; and the Boca Barra of San Francisco being cleared for the admission of large vessels; and both these ends are, in his opinion, attainable without having to overcome extraordinary difficulties.

No one ever visited the Goatzacoalcos without being impressed with the facility with which the whole of it might be made navigable. The stability of its bed is owing both to the slowness of the current, which prevents its excavating the bottom and banks, and to the clearness of the waters, which carry no materials down to make new deposits. The gentleness of the current may be inferred from the fact that its course, with all its windings from the confluence of the Malatengo to the sea, measures one hundred and sixty miles with a fall of only one hundred and thirty feet.

It has been observed that the bar of the Goatzacoalcos is permanent, and it is hoped that whatever works may be

*The abundance of ship timber which is to be found on the borders of the river itself, the convenience and security of the port, the facility of defending its entrance by placing batteries at the points of the river facing the channel, and which from the nature of the ground might be rendered unassailable from the land side, are all so many combining circumstances to render *the Goatzacoalcos the fittest place in all the Gulf of Mexico for the establishment of an arsenal.* These advantages were first pointed out to the Spanish government by the engineer Cramer, in the year 1774. In 1778 another engineer, Don Miguel del Corral, submitted to the Viceroy a plan for the construction of an arsenal, with two building slips for vessels of every size and a fort to defend the entrance of the river.

necessary to give greater depth to the river will have a permanent result, if they are well conceived and properly executed.

In some of the upper parts of the river it may perhaps be necessary to straighten its course, checking the increased current by means of a lock, and in others to construct solid embankments so as to limit the width of its bed.

To change the established course of a mighty river is one of the most delicate operations in hydraulics, and requires not only much skill and tact, but a careful study of local circumstances. The two most difficult points are the rapids of the old and new Mal Paso, where the river runs upon a rocky bed; but these are of limited extent, and the many efficient means employed in similar cases are too well known to allow of much importance being attached to such obstacles. With these two exceptions the remaining rapids are generally caused by shingle and sand-banks, and diminish gradually in number until they become very rare below the river Jumuapa.

After passing the small hill of Cuapinaloya, the Goatzacoalcos divides itself into two branches, called Apotzongo and Mistan. If the former of these were straightened, compelling at the same time the whole of the waters of the river to run through its channel, and obstructing the entrance of the other arm, the shoal of Horqueta would be removed, and the river become navigable for large vessels to a point beyond Cuapinoloya, namely, more than sixty-two miles from the mouth of the Goatzacoalcos.

Before dismissing this subject it is necessary to make one other observation. The various authors, who have spoken of the bar of the Goatzacoalcos, differ in their statements as regards its depth,

Dampier states it to be 14 English feet.
Cramer " 18 Castilian feet at mid-tide.
Orbegozo " 14 Castilian feet.
Robinson " 22 English feet, and more in the rainy season.
The last Commission 6,40 meters, or 21 English feet.

These apparent contradictions will disappear when we observe with Don Tadeo de Ortiz that the bar has two channels, the depth of one varying at different seasons of the year from eighteen to twenty-three feet, and that of the other from twelve to fifteen. It is not likely that all have measured the deepest channel, besides from the opportunity which Mr. Moro had of examining the plan of the soundings made by Cramer, he thinks, he may with certainty assert, that the bar has increased in depth.

If regulating the course of the Goatzacoalcos may be productive of some trouble, there would at all events be very little at the Pacific shore, in opening the shoal of the Boca Barra of San Francisco, and giving more depth to a canal in the lakes, the bottom of which is nothing but mud and shingle.

These difficulties once conquered, nothing would remain but to convey a sufficient quantity of water to an elevated point from whence it may be distributed and directed on the one side to the Goatzacoalcos, and on the other to the upper lagoon. Both objects may be attained by different means.

DIFFERENT PROPOSED LINES FOR THE CANAL.

First Project.—This would be to open a trench which would lead the waters of the Ostuta to the valley of the Chicapa, and another, which beginning a little above the "Ultimo Rancho," would direct the waters thus collected to the tableland of Tarifa, following the brows of the hills to the north of the valley watered by the upper Chicapa and the Monetza. These two proposed trenches are shown in the map. The point of distribution of the canal would be placed between the Cerro del Convento and the estate of Tarifa, from whence it would descend on the one side to the Goatzacoalcos, following nearly the natural course of the waters, and on the other would reach the upper lagoon, descending along the eastern and southern sides of the hills of Masahua by means of proper locks. The canal would have to be cut through a soil formed in some parts of an argillaceous rock of excellent quality, and in others of marl, clayish sand, and slates.

Second Project.—The second combination, undoubtedly easier and more economical than the preceding, would be to direct to the Portillo of Tarifa, that part of the canal which goes towards the Pacific, and from thence along the brow of the hills to the East, join the canal to the river Chicapa, which would be made navigable as far as the plain.

Mr. Moro, in his report, offers other solutions, so far as the extent of his trigonometrical operations could permit, and which, like the two projects which we have presented, are subject to modification or improvement, whenever we will be supplied with further information by a more detailed examination of the ground. It has appeared to us, however, best to give these several suggestions here, for the more intelligent comprehension of the subject, and we give them as we find them in his report.

Third Project.—Another method was suggested, that of converting into a lake the valleys of Chicapa, San Miguel and Monetza, for the collection of the waters of the Ostuta and Chicapa. This new *lake* would be at the same time an excellent basin for navigation, and well adapted for the distribution of the waters. The project would establish a port in the midst of the mountains, and avoid the deep excavation which would otherwise be required in the feeder to elevate the waters to the level of the Tarifa plain. It would, however, be necessary to examine whether the cost of the construction of the great dike, which would be required, would be inferior to that of the excavation.

Fourth Project.—It would, perhaps, be possible to make the dividing point of the waters in the valley of the Monetza by converting it into a reservoir. At the place where this little river flows into the Chicapa, it comes out through a narrow gorge between two mountains, so near each other that it would be easy to unite them by means of a dike, and which would doubtless be less expensive than the one called for by the preceding project. From this reservoir the waters could be supplied to either slope.

Fifth Project.—After having conveyed to the immediate

neighborhood of Tarifa the waters of the Ostuta and Chicapa, by the means shown in the first project, the next consideration would be to take advantage of the beds of the rivers, which from that point proceed towards both oceans, regularizing their courses so as to make them navigable. The stream of Tarifa, and the rivers Chichihua and Malatengo might be followed on the one side, and on the other the Monetza and the Chicapa.

It would not always be possible or convenient to follow the windings of the rivers, but by carefully observing the ground, considerable saving of labor might be effected in the work of excavation. The windings of the Monetza and Chicapa, judiciously turned to account, would give to the canal a more extensive line in which the locks could be better distributed. The solid rocks, through which these two rivers run, would afford, both at the bottoms and sides, a firm foundation to the necessary works.

DIMENSIONS OF THE WORK, AND ESTIMATE OF ITS PROBABLE COST.

Mr. Moro expresses himself in the following manner as to the amount of lockage in his projected canal:

"Selecting the proper ground, the fall of the proposed canal is:

From the table-land of Tarifa to Pacific..	660 feet.
From the same point to the mouth of the Malatengo,........................	525 "

Given to it a number of locks proportionate to that of the Caledonian Canal, there would be required:

On the side of the Pacific,...............	89 locks.
On the side of the Atlantic,.............	72 "
Total number of locks...................	161.

But the number of locks depends in a great measure on the accidental form of the ground; and, these permitting there might be given to each lock a fall of ten feet, in which case their number would be reduced:

On the Pacific side to....................	67
On that of the Atlantic to...............	53
In all....................................	120

However, to come nearer to the existing data, and because it might be necessary to put one or more locks below the confluence of the Malatengo, we will suppose that the total number of necessary locks is one hundred and fifty."

This may be too liberal an allowance, and it is probable that the result of a detailed survey and a careful location would be that the height of lockage would be reduced. We must not forget that we have not yet before us even an *avant projet*, and that a more detailed investigation may improve the nature of our information.

The length of the canal from the Goatzacoalcos to the Pacific, according to the first of the several projects and which presents the longest line, would be fifty miles.

Mr. Moro took for his model, in making his calculations, the Caledonian Canal. His canal like the Caledonian would thus be one hundred and twenty-two feet wide at the top and fifty feet at the bottom, with a depth of twenty feet. He says, "the canal which I have taken as a model, is the Caledonian, the dimensions of which appear to me sufficient. To alter them much would occasion a considerable increase in the expenditure, perhaps without a suitable compensation, whilst the alteration required in the dimensions of some of its parts for the admission of steamers destined to a transatlantic navigation would not make it much more expensive."*

"Although the Caledonian canal measures less than twenty-two English miles of proper channel, if we add to it the cost of cleansing and deepening the lakes, it may be con-

* The Caledonian canal, completed by M. Telfort in 1822, consists of several short canals, connecting together some lakes and thereby establishing a communication between the Atlantic ocean and the German sea.

sidered as twenty-five miles long. The declivity from the top of the canal is of a medium heighth of ninety-five feet on each side, and it has in all twenty-seven locks.

From the statement in the Encyclopædia Britannica (7th edition, vol. 19, page 750) it would appear that the above named canal cost up to 1822, when it was opened, the sum of £905,258, but as I find in other works that its total cost was £986,924, I will proceed with my calculation upon this last amount, although less favorable.

Each lock of the Caledonian canal cost upon an average £8,000, and therefore the whole twenty-seven amounted to £216,000. Deducting this sum from the total cost, it will appear that the twenty-five miles of canal cost, exclusive of the locks, £760,000 and each mile £30,000 or $150,000.

The trench, intended to convey to Tarifa the united waters of the Ostuta and Chicapa, would be about fifteen miles in length, and we will give to the section of its excavation four hundred and thirty superficial feet front. According to what is actually paid in Mexico and the United States for a similar work in soils analagous to that of the isthmus, its total cost will be about $2,000,000.

The trench necessary to join the Ostuta to the Chicapa might be three miles in length at the utmost, and allowing for unforseen obstacles in this part of the country on account of the nature of its rocks, we will suppose it to cost $600,000.

Lastly let us apply $800,000 more to regulate the course of the Goatzacoalcos and to excavate the lakes and the Boca Barra. Then, summing up the preceding calculations, the total amount of the work will be found to consist of the following sums:

Cost of 150 locks at $40,000	$6,000,000
" 50 miles of canal at $150,000,	7,500,000
" 15 miles of trench,	2,000,000
" 3 miles of trench,	600,000
Regulation of the Goatzacoalcos, lakes and Boca Barra,	800,000
Total cost,	$16,900,000"

It would be an error to suppose that every portion of the work must, in our case, cost more than it would in the United States. The prodigious quantity of timber of the best quality which lies profusely in every part through which the canal would pass; the excellent kinds of building stone, the lime, bitumen, clay and all other necessary materials which nature seems to have taken pleasure in scattering in the most convenient spots; and, lastly, the ground and the waters, the acquisition of which occasions often considerable expenditure, and which, in our case, if it did occasion any at all, would be so trifling as not even to be worth mentioning, are all advantages in favor of the undertaking. To these advantages we may add the facility of obtaining cheap labor from the population of the isthmus, which, without any doubt, will be the most convenient to be employed in constructing the canal.*

Mr. Moro does not take into consideration these different advantages, supposing them to be counterbalanced by other circumstances, and he therefore takes as a guide in his calculations the cost of an analogous undertaking, generally admitted to have been exceedingly expensive by a combination of adverse circumstances. He does more: he applies his calculations to the first project, which as has been mentioned may be considered as the most costly, and he supposes the necessity of excavating the whole of the canal from the confluence of the Malatengo to the lagoons, without taking advantage of any of the favorable accidents of the ground.

---

*Mr. J. J. Williams, who acted as principal assistant engineer in the survey of the isthmus of Tehuantepec, which was made in 1851 under General Barnard, and who published at that time a very well written book on the whole subject, gives sixty-one thousand as the population of the isthmus of Tehuantepec.

In order to complete our information concerning the resources offered, we insert here the following statistical table annexed to Mr. Moro's report of 1843:

Divisions.	Population.	Live Stock.		
	Inhabitants.	Cattle.	Horses and mules	Sheep.
Southern part of the isthmus,......	30,845	44,135	11,260	1,500
Northern part of the isthmus,.....	21,011	67,143	25,000	230
Total..................	51,856	111,278	36,260	1,730

CLIMATE OF THE ISTHMUS OF TEHUANTEPEC.

The question of climate is one of great importance with reference to the location of a ship-canal. M. Michel Chevalier, in examining, twenty-five years ago, the circumstances which ought to be kept in view, in selecting the most appropriate plan for an interoceanic communication, very justly observes that one of the most important is its salubrity. He says, in speaking of Panama: "However great might be the saving of time effected by steering through the isthmus, it would always be shunned by vessels if it were to prove a charnel-house."

We have already spoken of the dangerous character of the climate in the southern part of the Isthmus, and bearing in mind this, while comparing it with the region of Tehuantepec, we cannot but be struck by a strong contrast.

The climate of the isthmus of Tehuantepec varies according to its topography, which can be separated into three divisions. The first, watered by the Goatzacoalcos and its affluents, is that of the northern slope, extending from the base of the Cordilleras with a breadth of fifty miles to the Gulf, and known as the Atlantic plains; the second, that of the centre, is called the Mountain district; the third, is that of the southern slope drained by the Tehuantepec river, and comprising a territory extending from the Cordilleras to the sea, with a width of twenty miles, called the Pacific plains. The basin of the Goatzacoalcos is low, with an extremely fertile alluvial soil, covered by dense forests intersected by many rivers which are subject to occasional overflow. This part of the isthmus, though the least healthy, yet enjoys a high degree of salubrity and need not excite the fears of the stranger who settles there, or the traveller who passes through. Yellow fever is unknown. The Mountain district is equal in salubrity to the healthiest countries of Europe. Lastly, the basin of the Tehuantepec is nearly as healthy as the central plateau, only warmer.

There are but two seasons upon the isthmus of Tehuantepec, summer and winter. During the winter the thermometer falls, in November, to about 70° Fahrenheit in the day time, and about 55° in the night. In the season of greatest heat, in May and June, the thermometer varies only from 80° to 90°. This latter peculiarity may be accounted for by the situation of the isthmus immediately below the upper plateau of the Andes, from which the cooler air descends and tempers the heat. The rain falls from July to October. All this country is perfectly healthy and offers a strong contrast to the neighboring regions, such as Tabasco and Vera Cruz, on the Gulf, and Acapulco, Huatulco and the coast of Guatemala, on the Pacific. This may be caused by the configuration of the earth's surface which at this point forms a defile, swept by continuous currents of air from the North and from the South, which contribute materially to the preservation of the salubrity of the country.

CONCLUSION.

The subject of an interoceanic ship-canal is not now for the first time before the American public, and it is precisely for that reason that it is not generally well understood.

An important fact has marked the latter part of the past year. The isthmus of Suez, after efforts which had consumed ten years of time, was opened to navigation by means of a "thorough cut," admitting the waters of the two oceans which wash its shores. This achievement was so much the greater, as many had utterly despaired of its success. As soon as the Suez canal was opened to commerce, the idea of an American canal sprang into new life, but at this time the project of a passage across our continent did not come from Europe, it arose, on the contrary, in this country.

All previous projects for piercing the American isthmus had their birth in Europe, stimulated by the interests of European commerce, which sought, in the opening of such a passage, that shorter route to the Indies of which Columbus had already dreamed. In the first Chapter of this essay we have given an account of the explorations on our Isthmus caused by various European governments and corporations with the view of establishing some sort of interoceanic communication. As we have seen, the results of these investigations were not encouraging, and when, finally, it was found that the promoters of the Suez canal were advancing energetically to the accomplishment of their project, the idea of an American canal was abandoned.

During this time the ruling nation on this side of the Atlantic, aided by European immigration, developed with great rapidity, extending its territory to the shores of both oceans, and creating powerful interests which now demand the establishment of interoceanic communication. There is to-day no question of accomplishing a work which is called for by the convenience of Europe; we have to do with an American enterprise, to be made for the people of the United States.

We have, however, as a people, permitted ourselves to become singularly confused in attempting the elaboration of our project. Three things seem to have befogged us.

We do not seem, in the first place, to comprehend that the aspect of the whole question has undergone a change. We set to work to-day, as Europe did, thirty-five years ago, when searching for a passage which should serve the interests of their own commerce and without reference to ours. We seem to have an eye only to the requirements of the Old World, and proceed to the construction of a canal for our own use, precisely as if the work was not to be done for us at all. We must abandon this preconceived idea, which looks to the configuration of the continent, to decide the location of the canal. On the contrary, we have to ascertain what services our own commerce is to receive from the proposed work, according to its location at one point or another upon the Isthmus. The general question to be agitated, when we are establishing a new means of communication, is what method should be pursued to realize the greatest amount of advantage by the proposed improvement, and this we should do in the present case. In the third Chapter we indicate what is expected of a canal traversing our continent, the services it will render, and the effect of its location in one part of the Isthmus rather than another.

The second thing, which improperly influences our minds, is the desire to perform on our continent the precise feat which has been accomplished at Suez, or even to surpass it. That which we have said in the second Chapter concerning the Suez Canal may suffice to give a condensed idea of the conditions which existed on that isthmus with reference to construction, the method adopted, its cost, the commercial movement through that channel by reason of its geographical position, and the means by which the capital invested will be made productive.

On the other hand, the investigations made upon the American isthmus show that the establishment of a "thorough cut," like that at Suez, would be possible only in the southern part, the very place which is, for other reasons, the least commodious for our canal. Another point is also clearly apparent, although we have not yet received the official report of the new expedition which was lately occupied with the exploration of Darien,—this is, that the outlay required for the construction of a "thorough cut," in this region will be entirely out of proportion to the earnings which the canal can make. We understand perfectly well that it would be advantageous if water communication between the two oceans could be effected without locks, but when this is demonstrated to be impossible, at least without extravagant expenditure, and when it is also determined that the locality, where alone such a work could be made, does not satisfy the commercial and political interests of our country, we shall be compelled to surrender to necessity. We do not believe that our work will lose any of its glory because it would be dissimilar to that of Europe, or that our national *amour propre* would suffer seriously from that fact. Enthusiasm is a good thing, even when it affects the execution of a great national work, but there are some other things which have at least equal value. One is the gift of weighing all things carefully and coolly, and of selecting what is really the most worthy.

The third thing, which generally prevents our people from coming to a wise decision upon the question of location and the method of construction, is the confused idea entertained concerning the traffic destined to make the capital invested in the American canal productive. We forget, with reference to this point, that a canal with the same object already exists in another hemisphere, more available for Europe and Asia, and capable of rendering to them greater services than an American canal, in the midst of the transformation which is, at this moment, going forward in the character of shipping and the nature of the motive power employed. Everybody has a vague idea of the grand commercial movement between Europe and Asia amounting to millions of tons, and imagines that a large part thereof would naturally be conveyed by way of the American canal, because Europe, in former days, had devised the project of passing through our continent. But times have changed.

Nothing can be more hurtful than to adopt wrong ideas of the returns of any enterprise which is projected, particularly when, as in the present instance, the revenue calculated to be derived, must govern the amount of the capital to be employed. The commercial statistics given in the third Chapter of this essay afford sufficient data for our judgment of this question. These figures show what can be reasonably expected of an American canal, and not only enable us to decide upon the mode of executing the work, but also the amount of the capital which is to be invested. No mistake should be any longer possible.

The "thorough cut" not being practicable, we have to search in the northern part of the Isthmus for a suitable locality for the construction of a canal with locks. Two localities present themselves for that purpose, as we go from the south to the north. The one upon the isthmus of Nicaragua, the other upon the isthmus of Tehuantepec.

At the present time we are not sufficiently well informed as to the proper method of constructing a ship-canal at Nicaragua, nor as to the cost of such an undertaking. It may be that the investigations, now being made by the recent *concessionnaire* of that line, will lead to a favorable solution, and that this enterprise will attain that success which the intervention of such an eminent man as M. Michel Chevalier gives us reason to expect. At present, however, neither of the lines projected by the previous explorers seems to present in a higher degree the advantages which we require for the location of a ship-canal, than does that of Tehuantepec. The fourth Chapter of this essay is devoted to a presentation of the results of the explorations made by Mr. G. Moro in 1843, with the view of constructing a canal to the Pacific from the upper waters of the Goatza-coalcos flowing into the gulf of Mexico.

The existence on the southern part of the isthmus of Tehuantepec of a supply of water for a summit level, with a *minimum* of one thousand cubic feet per second, seems to be well established, and all that we know of the work of Mr. Moro makes us desirous of a more detailed investigation and survey, in order to ascertain if the dividing line of the waters can be determined in a satisfactory manner, and if a proper line can be selected to reduce the height of lockage indicated.

After having presented with a good deal of minuteness the results of the explorations of Mr. Moro, we have also described the project of the canal as he has suggested it, without, however, the intention of offering his conception as a model for execution. The ship-canal, to be constructed, must also be wider and deeper than indicated in the project of Mr. Moro who has taken for his example the Caledonian Canal with a depth of but twenty feet. A depth of from twenty-three to twenty-six feet, and a proportional width would be required. This modification, we think, would not raise the cost of construction to a figure out of proportion to the revenues to be obtained from the canal. Mr. Moro fixed the cost of his project at $17,000,000; suppose we add $17,000,000 more to construct a canal of more commodious dimensions with a good system of lockage, and to improve the navigation of the Goatzacoalcos, the work would cost $34,000,000. The enterprise would then be in a healthy financial condition, with a capital proportioned to the returns which it would be calculated to earn.

Our commercial statistics show at present a movement of at least one million and a half of tons, the greatest part of which would employ the future canal, without taking into account those of the sailing vessels, plying between Europe and Asia, which would prefer this new route. Suppose that the tariff would be of $2 per ton, there would be, from the beginning, an earning of about $3,000,000, besides other incidental items of revenue. Deducting the cost of operating, we find thus that the canal would have, from its very opening, an assured revenue, in view of which, the capitalist need not hesitate to invest in the enterprise.

All this, certainly, would be a more modest affair than the Suez Canal, but it would have the advantage of being carried forward to completion, and of becoming genuinely useful, while impossible projects and undertakings based upon a chimera fail, and retard for the whole human race the realization of practical and profitable enterprises.

FAC-SIMILE OF

MORO'S MAP OF THE SOUTHERN PART OF THE ISTHMUS OF TEHUANTEPEC,

Showing the line of the Ship Canal projected by him in 1843.

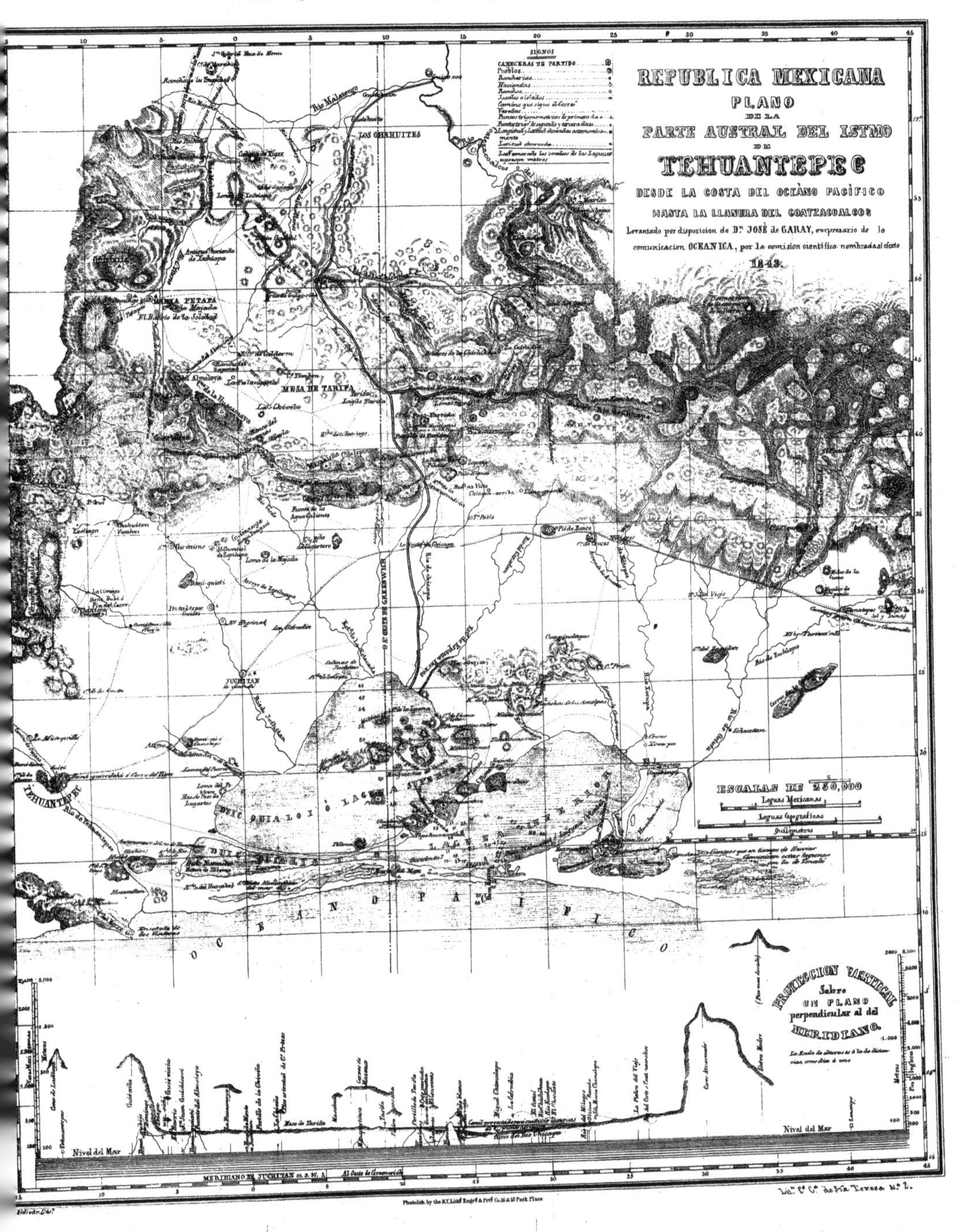

www.ingramcontent.com/pod-product-compliance
Lightning Source LLC
LaVergne TN
LVHW021411110826
845150LV00007B/1878

* 9 7 8 1 4 2 5 5 1 0 9 4 7 *